Praise for
Practice of the Presence: A Revolutionary
Translation by Carmen Acevedo Butcher

"In this radiant new translation, Carmen Acevedo Butcher puts her acclaimed skills as a translator fully in the service of her listening heart to deliver Brother Lawrence's timeless teaching on simplicity and presence to a world desperately in need of it. More than a translation, this is a *transmission*, conveying not only Lawrence's words but the spirit of inclusivity and kindness from which he wrote them. It is her faithfulness to the fragrance of his presence that makes her translation so inviting, even as we watch her take a few risks to reach a whole new world of seekers. It was a joy to watch Carmen and Brother Lawrence making such sweet music together."

—**Cynthia Bourgeault,** author of *The Heart of*
Centering Prayer, The Meaning of Mary Magdalene

"How to live in the presence of God is of the essence of the Christian mystical tradition. Few mystical texts have presented a practical method for attaining God's presence as effectively as the collection of letters, conversations, and biographical materials known as *The Practice of the Presence of God*, stemming from the Carmelite brother, Lawrence of the Resurrection (d. 1691). This gem of the Christian mystical tradition has now been made available in a striking new translation and study by Carmen Acevedo Butcher. It is a book to be treasured by all who are devoted to the inner life."

—**Bernard McGinn,** Naomi Shenstone
Donnelley Professor emeritus, Divinity School,
University of Chicago

"What a bold, vibrant, and potent translation of this mystical masterpiece! As she did with the perennial wisdom jewel *Cloud of Unknowing*, Carmen Acevedo Butcher once again breaks open the stilted and patriarchal language that encrusts our most life-giving spiritual treasures and makes the practice of the Presence easy to grasp and impossible to resist.

Its author, the humble seventeenth-century sage Brother Lawrence, reminds us that every task, no matter how ordinary, is a fresh opportunity for drawing near to the Friend. And that the more we take refuge in this intimacy, frequently repeating such phrases as 'My God, I am all yours,' or 'God of love, I love you with all my heart,' or 'Love, create in me a new heart,' the more often we find ourselves simply resting in the presence of Love Itself."

—**Mirabai Starr,** translator of John of the Cross,
Teresa of Ávila, and Julian of Norwich;
author of *God of Love* and *Wild Mercy*

"The greatest mystics, like Kabir and Rumi, have a simplicity and electric directness that both take our breath away and point us to the true north of our essential divine identity and the radiance of the divine presence in and as everything. Brother Lawrence is one of these universal visionaries, and reminds us relentlessly, in his soberly ecstatic and humble way, that what we search for with such anxiety and longing is always alive in us, and that the divine presence soaks and invigorates all things at all times. In a time of such devastation and rabid confusion, Brother Lawrence's testimony is of sublime help, and a source of radical encouragement to all seekers on all paths. In these wonderful, naked, luminous translations he lives afresh, inviting us with every word into the reality he knows and embodies so simply and fully. Do not miss this book, and give it to everyone you know."

—**Andrew Harvey,** author of *The Hope* and
Turn Me to Gold: 108 Translations of Kabir

"Carmen Acevedo Butcher's powerful translation of Brother Lawrence's *Spiritual Maxims*, letters, and conversations opens our hearts to experience God through the lens of a humble seventeenth-century friar, one who had very little to say about institutional religion and very much to say about the presence of God in the everyday lives of ordinary people. At a time when institutionalized religion often fails us, this translation reminds us that we are constantly surrounded by the divine presence and that God is accessible to us at any moment of life and far beyond the confines of churches, temples, and synagogues. It is a timely translation that holds enormous possibility for the reformation of a religious faith that desperately needs it."

—**Rob Nash,** associate dean for doctoral programs and
professor of comparative religion and mission,
McAfee School of Theology of Mercer University,
Atlanta, Georgia

"Carmen Acevedo Butcher brings scholarly expertise and abundant love to this fresh rendering of a classic work of Christian literature. Brother Lawrence's spiritual insights are as timely now as they were when first written centuries ago, making this beautiful translation a much-needed gift to the world today. With its inclusion of helpful historical and biographical context, this edition deserves a place in every personal and public library."

—**Karen Swallow Prior,** research professor of English and
Christianity & Culture, Southeastern Baptist
Theological Seminary; author of *On Reading Well:
Finding the Good Life through Great Books*

"Brother Lawrence, a seventeenth-century French monk, persists as a powerful force and resource in Christian tradition. His testimony, in letters and conversations, is marked by humility, vulnerability, simplicity, and a focus on love. In this welcome new edition Carmen Acevedo Butcher has made the work of Brother Lawrence freshly available in a most accessible and compelling way. In our world marked by speed, convenience, and hostility, no doubt Brother Lawrence is a persuasive antidote and alternative to a culture of alienation. We may be grateful to Acevedo Butcher for her careful, attentive work in this contemporary offer of ancient trustful wisdom."

—**Walter Brueggemann,** Columbia Theological Seminary,
author of *Money and Possessions*

"Presence, not often or easily practiced, is made, once more, available to us. Each of us can practice presence by embodying all that we inhabit.

May we come closer to ourselves and to God by a newly found practice of presence. This book is one such tool to inhabit a profound presence."

—**Robyn Henderson-Espinoza, PhD,**
author of *Body Becoming: A Path to Our Liberation*

"Acevedo Butcher's careful translation recreates the volatile, war-filled, plague-ridden world of seventeenth-century France. She invites us into the monastery kitchen with Brother Lawrence as he cleans the pots and pans amidst literal turmoil outside the monastery doors—a similar situation to what I imagine many of us find ourselves in today! This comprehensive translation of letters, maxims, and last words revolves around the simple practice of the presence, which is simply, and at its most essential, an awareness of the presence of God. Acevedo Butcher beautifully captures what Brother Lawrence continually reminds us: There are no special words, devotions, or actions needed, just simplicity of thought and deed."

—**Father Richard Rohr, OFM,**
Center for Action and Contemplation

"Brother Lawrence is not only a great Christian mystic; he's also charming and accessible—a sage whose wisdom is thoroughly down-to-earth and relevant to today. Carmen Acevedo Butcher's fresh, richly embodied, and at times surprising translation makes the words of this Carmelite contemplative truly come alive."

—**Carl McColman,** author of *Eternal Heart* and
The Big Book of Christian Mysticism

"Carmen Acevedo Butcher listens across the centuries and finds a companion for all of us in a disabled, veteran of war, shoe-mending, soup-making monk. Brother Lawrence's 'sacred, ordinary, and necessary' way of prayer can help all of us to pause, and more importantly, to bring our minds back to love. This translation is a joyful conversation with Brother Lawrence, one in which we can all participate."

—**Kaya Oakes,** author of *The Defiant Middle*

"In these pages, I sat across from a blue-collar saint whose temple is a kitchen. Brother Lawrence has bequeathed to us that rare wisdom that weds the celestial to the terrestrial. He teaches us how to punctuate the ordinary tasks of life with petition, thanksgiving, and the practice of standing in the presence of Jesus, even as he flips omelets for the Almighty. This splendid book, exquisitely written and scintillating with wisdom, will breathe divine life into the sacred ordinary of the Christian."

—**Chad Bird,** Scholar in Residence at 1517

"The best translations of spiritual classics are not those that sound familiar but those that strike the ear in a whole new way, because they offer proof that the teachings are still alive and evolving in our own day. Whether you love the teachings of Brother Lawrence or have never encountered them before, you can trust Carmen Acevedo Butcher to offer you a fresh hearing that is in tune with the lives we are living right now."

—**Barbara Brown Taylor,** author of *An Altar in the World*

"As time goes on, new translations of classic works are desirable. Carmen Acevedo Butcher has provided one for our times. Her work reflects her love of Brother Lawrence and her familiarity with the practice of the presence of God. Her comprehensive version is extensive and full."

—**Father Salvatore Sciurba, OCD,**
Discalced Carmelite Friars, Monastery of
Our Lady of Mount Carmel, Washington, DC

"Many have an acquaintance with Brother Lawrence, but Carmen Acevedo Butcher helps us to know him far better in this new translation. We not only experience a fresh, contemporary, and accessible translation of *The Practice of the Presence of God*, but we also get a greater understanding of this legendary yet simple man who guides us on a path of contemplation of the greatest love of all."

—**Vincent Bacote,** director of the Center for Applied
Christian Ethics, and professor of theology, Wheaton College

"Carmen Acevedo Butcher has given us a careful and luminous translation of a spiritual classic. This great book still has the power to bring us into the Presence."

—Don Brophy, author of *One Hundred Great Catholic Books*

"Carmen Acevedo Butcher's insightful and inclusive translation of Brother Lawrence's classic, *The Practice of the Presence of God*, is such a needed balm for our beleaguered souls. Its wisdom reminds us that the maelstrom of this present age is not unique. In this world we will have trouble—for example, pandemics, environmental disasters, and severely strained social contracts—but they are transitory distractions. Acevedo Butcher's spiritually attuned translation invites us to host presence, awaken hope, and immerse ourselves in love."

—Rev. Dr. Barbara A. Holmes,
president emerita, United Theological Seminary of the
Twin Cities; core faculty for the Center for
Action and Contemplation

"This is Presence come alive for a new generation, for our conflicted spirits. Reveals the most durable way of prayer not dependent on words I've ever found. Highly recommended!"

—Jon M. Sweeney, author of
Nicholas Black Elk and *Feed the Wolf*

"To live guided by true presence. To pray as an invitation to embodied authenticity. To orient heart and mind in the direction of kindness. This is the theology of Brother Lawrence brought alive in this beautiful translation of *The Practice of Presence* by Carmen Acevedo Butcher. Accessible and freshly relevant, the book is a bell of mindfulness to accompany readers in deeper contemplation, making it an important guide to self-understanding, spiritual exploration, and unity. Pause as you read. Breathe. Practice presence. Allow this profoundly invitational book to settle into your heart."

—Valerie Brown, JD, MA, PCC,
Dharma teacher, Plum Village; faculty, Georgetown University,
School of Continuing Studies; author of *Hope Leans Forward*

"Every skilled translator knows only too well the looming meaning of the French phrase *Traduire, c'est trahir*—'To translate is to betray.' The phrase means that something essential in the original language is left out of the translation. The translator's art requires two skills at once. She must indwell each language while at the same time listening deeply and waiting patiently. Carmen Acevedo Butcher, both delicate and precise as embroidery, is no traitor. With inspiring, poetic prose she provides us the first complete translation of all Brother Lawrence's works. And she does this from a unique perspective. As a woman of color, she is sensitive to the need to look beneath the pot-scrubbing Brother Lawrence (he actually detested the work) to see the social constraints that bore upon the man, Nicolas Herman, who, in King Louis XIV's France, was socially excluded for not being adequately French in quite the right way. Carmen Acevedo Butcher gives a living voice to a person who did not count in his own culture. Out of this place of not-counting emerges a depth of spiritual wisdom that transcends the ages. Carmen Acevedo Butcher is uniquely positioned to give him a voice in a way no previous translator has. Her translation will be the new standard by which other translations will be measured.

—**Martin Laird, OSA,** professor of
Early Christian Studies, Villanova University;
author of *Into the Silent Land*; *A Sunlit Absence*;
and *An Ocean of Light* (all by Oxford University Press)

"A vibrant, urgent, and earthy translation of a timeless classic."
—**James Martin, SJ,** author of *Learning to Pray*

"Imagine Mr. Rogers was a mystic. That will give you a sense of the warm spiritual heart of Brother Lawrence, brought to life for the twenty-first century in this vivid, timely new translation. In our age of distraction and despair, Brother Lawrence's counsel to practice the presence of Love is not a method or a formula, but the gentle gift from a friend of the God who is our Friend. This is a book to cherish as God's incessant invitation to draw near."

—**James K. A. Smith,** author of *You Are What You Love:
The Spiritual Power of Habit*

"To be present to God: this is the 'method without method' experimented by a humble Parisian religious of the seventeenth century. This new translation, faithful to the original text, allows us to rediscover a simple spiritual path accessible to all."

—**Denis Sureau,** editor, theologian, author of
Frère Laurent de la Résurrection:
Le cordonnier de Dieu (Artège, 2020)

BY NICOLAS HERMAN,
BROTHER LAWRENCE
OF THE RESURRECTION

PRACTICE
OF THE
PRESENCE

TRANSLATED
BY CARMEN ACEVEDO BUTCHER

BROADLEAF BOOKS
MINNEAPOLIS

PRACTICE OF THE PRESENCE
A Revolutionary Translation by Carmen Acevedo Butcher

Cover design: Studio Gearbox

Print ISBN: 978-1-5064-7860-9
Book ISBN: 978-1-5064-7861-6

Printed in Canada

To the Women's Prison Association

The Women's Prison Association (WPA) is the first US
organization for women impacted by incarceration.
Since 1845 WPA has innovated programs that address
women's histories of trauma, mental health needs, parental
stress, and other factors that can lead to systems involvement.
Together they reunify families, develop workplace skills and
build careers, access health care, and find safe, affordable
housing. WPA is a nonprofit located in New York City's
East Village. Visit wpaonline.org, and follow @wpa_nyc on
Instagram and Twitter. The women at a maximum-security
prison befriended this book's translator when at nineteen she
volunteered there for three months. They are still remembered.

A generous donation from the proceeds from each copy of
Practice of the Presence
goes directly to WPA in support of
their advocacy for women.

Brother Lawrence was uneducated and rough by nature yet wise and sensitive by grace. This mixture was lovable and showed us God in him.... You have seen many wise people taught by Love. They had no formal training in theology. No human teacher was involved. Is it any wonder that Love teaches us to love? Those who love sincerely, and who become intoxicated with the new wine of the Spirit speak an entirely new language.

François Fénelon

I'm only asking you to look at Love, even if just for a moment.... Practice this mindfulness, no matter how distracted you feel. ... You have the power to become accustomed to this practice.... Stay with such a good Friend as long as you can.

Teresa of Ávila

There is in you something that waits and listens for the sound of the genuine in yourself. ... Now there is something in everybody that waits and listens for the sound of the genuine in other people.... Can you find a way to hear the sound of the genuine in yourself?

Howard Thurman

CONTENTS

GROUNDED IN LOVE

A TRANSLATOR'S
PERSONAL NOTE

Here is how I first discovered the spirit of the practice of the presence. Walking down the steamy, weedy shoulder of Highway 20, cicadas buzzing, and my mind, I had no destination in rural northwest Georgia. Semis and cars whizzed by inches near, but I didn't care. I wandered hours, often, head bowed, shoulders slumped by a heavy burden of depression then. I tried forever, learning I couldn't fix the slumping, how trauma torques the body. But then decades on, I did find help somehow, a kind doctor, counselor, therapy, and words to name my pain, even begin healing, learn how to stand tall on the inside at least, but on that June day, I was lost and lonely, when I looked up to see a book flat on its back on the gray tarmac, cream-colored pages facing blue sky and waving back and forth in the speed of exhaust-fumes at tire level. It looked abandoned.

I ran out in the middle of the busy road to rescue it. Hardback, it had a dark black tread on the inside of its front flap. But all pages were intact. What that book was and what it taught me are a story for another day. The magic of it is this:

Standing in the red dust on the side of that road, I read words on a random page in that book-likely-whooshed-off-a-distracted-owner's-car-roof, and knew I'd found a friend.

Some time later, I would read that book's fascinating introduction, I'd learn everything I could about the author and what else they'd written, and I'd study everything associated with that book.

All that mattered on that day, though, was the first random page opened for me. Every sentence, every word, all that rhythm, every idea, and joy, and difficulty, and human longing, all of that needed nothing to speak for them, not an introduction, not an author's note.

If this translation of *Presence* were now decades later mindlessly left on someone's car roof and blew off, I hope that anyone chancing on it would pick it up, and even if it smelled of gas fumes or had a tire mark from, say, a logging truck, they would read a few words anywhere in it and think, *I've found a friend.*

Also I hope they would experience, in the middle of pain, and emptiness, like Brother Lawrence, the strange gift of divine presence, Love. Sometimes that is as curious as a random good book lost in the middle of a busy road. It often happens in a time of darkness. When Brother Lawrence was simply looking at a barren tree one day, he felt hope for his humanness, and divine acceptance, and from that profound encounter grew his relationship with Kindness. Over time, he experienced ordinary moments as extraordinary peace and love.

What is this book, this practice of the presence? Brother Lawrence just calls it *the presence*. It is a form of micro-prayer done on the fly. A mini-conversation with God. A brief "lifting up of the heart."

Done anywhere, anytime, the practice is perfect for anyone. We can't fail at it. It's shorter than a tweet. It takes less time than sending a text. It's easy, Brother Lawrence says: "In the middle of your tasks you can comfort yourself with Love as often as you can." The presence is for all people everywhere: "Everyone is capable of these familiar conversations with God.... Love knows what we can do," the friar says.

"Let's begin."

INTRODUCTION

TO *PRACTICE OF THE PRESENCE*

FEATHERS AND THE FRIAR'S GROUNDED WISDOM

Birds, trees, insects, sheep, and chamber pots helped make this book.

The slit nib of a quill pen held in the writer's hand was its beginning. Crafted from a molted flight feather of a swan or a goose, this pen used ink that eighty-foot oaks and quarter-inch wasps made possible. By laying eggs on oak leaf buds, these tiny insects caused the growth of marble-sized plant orbs called galls that grew in weeks of silent transformation until matured wasps chewed out and flew off, and then these galls, rich in tannins, were picked, dried, pestled, soaked, and processed to make good ink.

Brother Lawrence's quill pen dipped in oak-gall ink skated over—and scratched on—the paper for three to six words at a time, in a flowing script like bâtarde rather than ronde, before his pen needed redipping. Blessed with ink, the penned pages grew.

When this handwritten manuscript arrived at the Parisian printer's shop in 1692, it was transformed. First its cursive words were transferred to tiny metal blocks. Left to right and upside down each letter or type was put on a tray, one by one and row on row, a slow process. After these were set in forms, a glossy black paste was spread on an ink block with a slice. Then strong hands took up the handles of two inking balls, or dabbers wrapped in untanned sheepskin, and rocked these pads on the ink block to diffuse the black ink, then smacked and dabbed their oily sticky leather evenly onto the printing surface. Their thump-thump-thump was the bassline of the work. The dabbers carried a pungent smell, soaked at night in a bath of urine to keep the sheepskin soft.

It seems felicitous that this book's quiet embodied wisdom began public life in a loud reeking printer's shop, and started privately with a once-blue-sky-soaring feather.

THE COMPLETE BROTHER LAWRENCE

Pages pressed, hung to dry, folded, cut, gathered, sewn, trimmed, backed, and covered, this book emerged quietly at the end of a century deafened by disaster and death. At a humble height of seven inches, by four-and-a-half across, and with its unknown author a year since dead, it could easily have disappeared from history. It was only published because, as often happens, a friend thought it ought to be.

Yet millions read and reread it, keeping this book in print across five centuries. It has proven evergreen for its Presence. The first edition was the size of a hand because readers wished to hold it, carry it with them.

Its Spirit drew people to it. The pull of the book's kind heart continues, and calls for a new, authentic, accurate, robust, and inclusive translation for our day.

This present edition offers a wide range of readers access for the first time to the complete Brother Lawrence. Based on books housed in the Bibliothèque Nationale de France, this translation includes all works from the two-part first edition: 1692's *Note to the Reader, Eulogy* (here *Last Words*), *Spiritual Maxims*, and *Letters*, and 1694's *The Ways* (here *Profile*), *Conversations*, and *The Practice of the Presence of God* (here *The Heart of Brother Lawrence*).

The original editions have a revolutionary theme of kindness and love. My translation of the French and reframing of its teaching are equally revolutionary. The translation was created with you in mind. Its concise wisdom is intended for everyone who seeks more peace and a better quality of life. If you crave more love in your day-to-day existence, as I do, and really, who doesn't, this is the book.

THE METHODLESS METHOD

At a quiet monastery nestled among fields and gardens on the shrinking outskirts of Paris, Brother Lawrence put his quill pen to paper, and described the practice of the presence as "*la plus facile*," "the easiest" form of prayer, and "*la plus efficace*," "the most effective." Central within his writing is this: anyone who wants to do it can, and will discover benefit.

One reason the friar's practice of the presence prayer is easy is that it's flexible and portable. Discalced (or "Shoeless") Carmelites call it "the methodless method." That's a good handle, for this practice knows life is chaotic. A prayer cushion isn't a requirement. To do the presence prayer, anyone can pause at any time, if they wish, for a micro-moment of rest with Love. We can say whatever's on our mind, ask for love, share worry, be mad, give thanks, feel wonder, ask for help, or just be. There's no scorecard of how many times a day we do it, no grade of *A, B, C*. This ordinary practice brings friendship with Kindness, joy, and self-compassion. The practice is also an exciting, daily spiritual experiment.

Brother Lawrence gives ordinary names to this prayer that connected him with Love's mystery. He calls it: "*la pratique de cette présence*," "the practice of this presence"; "*la présence de Dieu*," "the presence of God"; "*la présence amoureuse*," "the loving presence"; "*cet exercice de la présence*," "this exercise of the presence"; and "*ce saint exercice*," "this sacred exercise." When he chooses the French word *exercice* for this practice, it echoes our own understanding of exercise, like a walk around the block or any stretching routine, invisible exercises build unseen flexibility.

The difficulties of his life and his own pain were material for his practice. And his experiences and the times in which he lived resonate in strong ways with our own. For a world in suffering, climate crisis, violence in the name of religion or power, and screens that often usurp human presence, his prayer practice is for us, now.

THE FRIAR OF POTS AND PANS

The friar's soulful life that continues through this book gives meaning to his monastic name, Brother Lawrence *of the Resurrection*. The lived wisdom of his faith unfolds into now, reanimating, green. Because he has long been a beloved spiritual guide, sometimes his true presence has been obscured by the adulation sustaining the image and icon of him as the humble friar.

This book presents him in more fullness, in his humanity. We witness his transformation by prayer. We see the young Lorrainer Nicolas Herman, a struggling, anxious, and wounded war veteran, become Brother Lawrence, a wise, calm friar who spent fifty years in a monastery, forty of those as a kitchen worker and thirty as a sandal repairer, with some overlap.

As I translated words and phrases, I imagined the chaotic activity that filled his kitchen with its steaming pots and hot ovens, several people talking to him at once, asking questions, giving directions, a friendly cacophony of soup-stirring spoons scraping metal bottoms, lids clattering. I saw him with his ever-present limp as he moved around the kitchen. I wondered how much his leg hurt. I mused over whether, when he was just a young cook in training, someone snapped at him impatiently for daydreaming: "Hand me that ladle quick, lad. Stop dawdling." I considered how, as principal cook for so many years of a restaurant-sized operation, he would carefully plan food for a monastery of friars, and juggle adding potatoes to the pot for visitors who just showed up.

As I reread and rethought how much Brother Lawrence disliked this kitchen work, I related to him. Anyone who has felt trapped in or overwhelmed by a job feels a kinship here. For this scullery work, he had the "strongest natural aversion," "*plus grande aversion naturelle*," as one of his best friends said, adding that the friar "got used to doing everything" there "for the love of God" by "asking in every situation for the grace to do this work," so "he found it very easy" during his fifteen years as head cook, from about age thirty-one to forty-six.

The friar's attitude resembles that of sixteenth-century mystic Teresa of Ávila, who often reminded her sisters: "Whenever you must do external work, like in the kitchen, remember God lives among the pots and pans, helping you" (*Foundations*). The more we read Teresa, the more we see her influence in him, and we remember that as the friars ate their communal meals in the refectory, they heard her works read aloud to them.

NICOLAS HERMAN AND KING LOUIS XIV

When this book first came out, Louis XIV was the most powerful ruler in western Europe. He dominated France. During the simple days of our cook/sandal maker/friar, the self-named Sun King enlarged the absolutist monarchy's muscle, and famously built the glittering palace complex at Versailles. Yet for real enduring power, millions keep returning to the spiritual direction of an author who never saw one word published while he was alive.

Nicolas Herman, whose monastic name after age twenty-six was Brother Lawrence of the Resurrection, lived and died in obscurity. And the seventy-seven years of his life were filled by the harrowing events of the seventeenth century.

Being born Nicolas Herman came with disadvantages in 1614 France. The social and political hierarchy of Christian Europe from the fifteenth through eighteenth centuries was rigid and deadly for some, and privileged and cushy for others. Your birth mostly determined your estate, and your estate, your life. The Ancien Régime in France was a threefold, man-made system often promoted and preached as divinely ordered.

The First Estate, the clergy, was divided into a higher bracket of those born into nobility and a lower one of those not. The clergy was generally under 1 percent of the entire population, but as the greatest of all corporations, the Church had the most vested interests to promote.

The Second Estate, the nobility, made up about 1 to 2 percent of the population. The Third Estate, about 98 percent of all living souls, included those considered commoners, urban and rural. These were the bourgeoisie, wage laborers, and peasants.

The powerful role of wealth in society presented grave problems for many. And Nicolas Herman was born into this system's third place.

NO COUNTRY, NO EDUCATION

Herman was also born with no country. His birthplace was the small village of Hériménil in the independent duchy of Lorraine, not annexed by France for 150 years. That made him a Lorrainer, not a Frenchman. To reach Paris from Hériménil took six long days by horse, traveling west.

When Nicolas Herman was born to Dominique Herman and Louise Majeur, he entered the world in the middle of nowhere, with no money and no social position. We only know his parents' names because these earned a one-line mention in a dusty, early eighteenth-century monastic record. Herman was not someone expected to be remembered. His parents, Dominique and Louise, did however give him a promising name. He would eventually, after many defeats, somehow manage to fulfill it: *Nicolas*, "victory of the people," from the Greek *nikē* and *laos*.

Like so many people today who want to learn, improve their lives, and contribute to their communities, but who lack the basic resources owing to pervasive inequities, he had no preordained opportunity for a quality formal education. However, if a Nicolas Herman applied to a university today as a first-year student, his strength of intellect, thoughtfulness, and community spirit would strongly recommend his acceptance. At the start of the seventeenth century, however, few choices existed for someone of his station.

WAR, PLAGUE, LITTLE ICE AGE

Herman was also born into a time of war. From age four until thirty-four, he lived while the Thirty Years' War raged through central Europe. This devastating series of religious civil wars began between Roman Catholics and Protestants and quickly expanded to include land grabs and profiteering. Eventually the Thirty Years' War involved most central European nations and territories.

It became infamous as one of Europe's deadliest wars. Killing became an industry, involving not only national armies but also armed marauders and mercenary troops. It perpetrated long-lasting tragedies of plundering and unimaginable violence toward civilians. It brought scourges of hunger and disease. The human losses have proven impossible to count, much less process. To contemplate its incomprehensible scale, some estimate that these three decades claimed the lives of 500,000 soldiers and eight million lives including civilians. That is one individual soul lost eight million times. Its repercussions are still felt today.

Ten years into this Thirty Years' War, France also knew the first of three bubonic plague epidemics in the seventeenth century. Historian Geoffrey Parker in *Global Crisis* estimates French deaths that century by plague were two million. The initial epidemic was the most widespread, affecting the whole country from 1628 to 1631. Nicolas was a teenager when the Black Death spread throughout the country.

Five years later France's second plague epidemic of that century occurred, lasting a year. And some three decades on, the plague returned for yet another year. Herman lived through plague in his teens, twenties, and fifties. Quarantine restrictions were mandated, reducing the spread and timeline of each successive wave.

In his lifetime Herman also experienced five decades of destructive global climatic conditions, where one-third or more of the entire human population perished. Climatologists call this period from 1640 to 1690 the Little Ice Age. It had the coldest weather on record in over one thousand years, and winters of six months or more brought unusually heavy snowfalls, followed by spring floods when the snows finally melted. The Seine burst its banks regularly, flooding Parisians' houses. Crops failed. Millions starved.

FIVE FEET AND THREE INCHES

A gilded government mishandled this cataclysmic Little Ice Age and the economic stagnation after the Thirty Years' War. Taxes were imposed on starving citizens who revolted in the streets, shouting, "No kings! No princes!" The incalculable suffering of this century warrants an entire chapter in Parker's *Global Crisis*, titled: "France in Crisis, 1618–88"—dates that nearly match the 1614–1691 life span of Nicolas Herman, Brother Lawrence.

Starvation was so prevalent among the Third Estate that its effects showed visibly. Of thousands enlisting in Louis XIV's army, men born in famine years between 1666 and 1694 had an average height of only five feet and three inches, the lowest on record in France. This "stunting" from starvation also damaged the development of major organs and immune systems of those living in the Third Estate, leaving malnourished children more vulnerable to contagious and chronic diseases.

These grim facts manifested in other ways. Frequently noblemen of this period are described rather loftily as "tall," which belies a complex social reality, where increased physical stature often marked a well-fed childhood, good health, and also seventeenth-century social status.

NINETEEN AND A SOLDIER

Within these social realities, Nicolas Herman decided to enter the heinous Thirty Years' War as a soldier at around the age of nineteen. A young man from an impoverished background and with no social or political advantages would likely see this move as providing him with food, structure for his days, and a stipend. Also, the French took control of the independent duchy of Lorraine in 1634 until 1661, possibly influencing his decision as a Lorrainer to join the local militia. During his short military career he performed many mindless marches and delivered messages.

He also became a prisoner of war. Captured and arrested by advancing German troops from Bernard of Saxe-Weimar's army, he was accused of spying, and threatened with death. Years later he told this harrowing story to his good friend Joseph of Beaufort, a Parisian priest who in the *Last Words* of this book describes how Herman escaped this dangerous situation.

INJURIES IN WAR

In 1635 at the siege of Rambervillers, young Herman was badly wounded in his leg. When the Duke of Lorraine launched an attack against the French there to regain this lost territory, Herman was likely among the troops that broke through town walls on August 10 and took back Rambervillers. Though hurt, he somehow made it the thirty kilometers north and home to his parents in Hériménil. And at about twenty-one he quit the military. This leg injury persisted the rest of his life, and he lived with pain and a limp from then on.

Beaufort says in *Last Words* that his friend lived "simply and with integrity" while in the military. Just as we have few details of his childhood and teenage years, we don't know what else may have happened during Herman's soldiering in the Thirty Years' War. But we see signs in this book that his military period caused him profound anguish, for reasons unknown, whether the atrocities of combat he may have witnessed or the guilt he may have carried. Historians' accounts of this war's violence and trauma recall our still inchoate understanding of complex post-traumatic stress disorder experienced by soldiers and civilians, and how many suffer in silence.

Les Grandes Misères et les Malheurs de la Guerre, usually abbreviated to *The Miseries of War*, a set of eighteen miniature etchings from 1633 by the Lorraine printmaker Jacques Callot, witnesses to the "astonishing bodily suffering" of the Thirty Years' War and its "total and pervasive" trauma, as professor Hillary L. Chute says in *Disaster Drawn*.

Beaufort shares that his friend "often relived in his mind the dangers of his days in military service, and the emptiness and corruption of the times." We read that Herman spent years "meditating on the disorders of his youth" ("*méditant les désordres de sa jeunesse*") and that these caused him "horror" ("*l'horreur*").

Many times we hear he "asked forgiveness" ("*demandait pardon*"), "resolved to give himself completely to God, and to change and to atone for his past conduct" ("*qu'il prit résolution de se donner tout à Dieu et de rectifier sa conduit passée*"), and did all he could to make amends or "atonement" ("*la satisfaction*").

A FAILED HERMIT AND A LOWLY FOOTMAN

After leaving military service, Herman tried the life of a religious hermit for a brief period, and, as Beaufort explains, he failed at it. It did not suit him, or perhaps he was not ready for it. Beaufort describes this turbulent hermitage experience intimately, saying that his friend "watched joy, sadness, peace, worry, passion, distraction, confidence, and despair, one after another, dominate his own soul." Every day he experienced emotional upheavals. Beaufort gently observes that while the hermit's life is "excellent for consideration by the advanced and the mature, . . . it is rarely best for beginners."

So Herman became a lowly footman for Monsieur Gaspard of Fieubet (1577–1647), the baron of Launac and royal treasurer of savings in Paris. Working for Fieubet introduced him to those of the Second Estate. A nobleman, Fieubet held a high government position collecting the royal domain's revenues and taxation and controlling the monarchy's revenues and expenditures.

For the former soldier, these were difficult days. When three decades later he looked back at his life as a young footman, he referred to himself as "a clumsy oaf who broke everything." In August 1666, when he was fiftysomething, he had the first of several conversations at the monastery with Father Joseph of Beaufort. In those the friar revealed feelings of failure from his twenties.

Beaufort recorded these *Conversations* carefully, preserving them. We can imagine his quill pen dipping into a pot of brown-black oak-gall ink, and writing the phrase he'd heard spoken: *un gros lourdaud qui cassait tout*: "a clumsy oaf who broke everything."

A CLUMSY OAF

As a footman or *laquais* (*lackey*), Herman believed himself "*un gros lourdaud*," "a clumsy oaf." That implies fiasco, for someone who understood his low status within his role and the expectations put on him. Something we recognize in status and structures today.

The friar's "*gros lourdaud* / clumsy oaf" is often glossed over as a sound bite for his humility, and his self-effacing phrase has lost much of its significance. Yet it's important and worthwhile to reclaim its meaning. His words remind us of the cruel inequities of the catastrophic seventeenth century. While the aesthetic of height and poise accorded with the upper echelons of Louis XIV's court, *gros* reflected the low rung of its hierarchy.

Gros, or *gross* in English, is often slang for "repulsive." In France in the mid-1600s, *gros* translates as "clumsy," and has a wide range of related negative connotations: "big, large, thick, fat; heavy, sad, weighty; rustic, lumpish, ignorant, untaught, lowborn, surly; inelegant, unpolished, awkward, clownish."

These connotations surface in an August 5, 1700, letter written by the archbishop of Cambrai, François Fénelon (1651–1715), to Marie Gruyn de Valgrand, countess of Montbéron. When depicting the friar, the archbishop chooses *grossier*, a variant of Brother Lawrence's own word, to mean "uneducated, unsophisticated, coarse, rough": "Brother Lawrence was uneducated and rough [*grossier*] by nature yet wise and sensitive by grace. This mixture was lovable, and showed us God in him."

Fénelon's intended praise and Brother Lawrence's self-selected *gros* "clumsy, large, untaught, lowborn," seem found, fossilized indictments of seventeenth-century inequities. In choosing *lourdaud,* "oaf," Brother Lawrence also brings in an insulting way of saying "not noble-born." Cotgrave's 1611 French-English dictionary has a long list of unflattering nouns for *lourdaud,* including "sod, dunce, grotesque, or a lout."

With possible roots in words for "bruising" (*lurid*) and "hunchback" (*lordós*), *lourdaud* largely sums up the unjust lives of the Third Estate. They starved, literally grew less tall as a result, and had heavy, bruising, back-breaking burdens placed on them, and those in other Estates referred to them in mainly derogatory terms.

This was the friar's lot at twenty. His chosen epithet of "a clumsy oaf" also brings an understanding of the Estate system, where he has just the right amount of irreverent spirit, a spirit that Nicolas Herman needed to persist and actualize a self, since he started down at the lowest level of society.

WHO BROKE EVERYTHING

The rest of the friar's self-description reveals more about his early life. In conversation with Beaufort, he recalls that as a young footman, he was a clumsy oaf "who *broke* everything": "qui *cassait* tout."

His *cassait* intimates a breaking of more than actual dishes. "I *shake* repeatedly, I *shatter,* or I *agitate*" is its Latin root, *quasso. Cassait* in many ways applies to how Herman felt at twenty about his career, physical-and-emotional health, and life: "broken, crushed in pieces, quashed; discharged, turned out of service; annulled, canceled." "Qui *cassait* tout," "who *broke* everything" suggests a profound anxiety that characterizes his twenties.

At this low point in Herman's life, an uncle became his mentor. Anonymized in *Last Words,* he was Herman's Uncle Jean, his mother's brother, also a native of Hériménil. Some years earlier, we also know, Jean Majeur had become a Discalced Carmelite lay brother.

Even with Jean's support, young Herman seemed stuck: "Day after day passed," and he "became more and more uncertain" about what to do with his life, as Beaufort discloses. Only after an indefinite period of "intense reflection, hard inner struggles, tears, and sighs," and "self-doubt" did Herman decide at twenty-six, in mid-June 1640, that he would enter the Order of the Discalced Carmelites on the Rue Vaugirard in Paris, as a lay brother himself.

A BARREN TREE IN WINTER AND A DARK NIGHT OF THE SOUL

But that was not the start of his spiritual life. Eight years before his decision to enter the monastery, eighteen-year-old Herman had had a profound religious experience. He shared it with his friend Beaufort in their first conversation. One day that winter, a year after the first bubonic plague of his lifetime had subsided, Herman was looking at a leafless, barren tree, when he realized suddenly and intensely that soon its "leaves would reappear, green," and then its flowers and fruits. This moment "lifted him up suddenly to God," and he "received a profound awareness of God's kindness and power that never left his soul."

Further intensifying this experience, four years earlier when Brother Lawrence was fourteen, France had had "a year without a summer." Low temperatures left many crops unripened, and people starved. After this, seeing green meant life to him in concrete ways. He said this mystical experience of spring gave him "such a love for God" that "he could not say it had ever increased" over the decades. As often happens in life, that had not made for a direct path for him to certainty or to the monastery.

For readers of *Practice of the Presence*, meeting Nicolas Herman means meeting every floundering soul. He knew anxiety and years of worry. He had an untamed mind. He had a guilty conscience. He felt estranged from God, love, purpose, and meaning.

He wrote about his decade-long dark night of the soul, from his mid-twenties to mid-thirties, and his descriptions of that floundering and his soul movement in *Presence* make for powerful reading in this book.

THE MONASTERY AT 74 RUE DE VAUGIRARD

Readers also witness the healthy spiritual formation and healing that occurred as Nicolas Herman, Brother Lawrence lived and worked for half a century in the large Paris monastery at the intersection of 21 Rue d'Assas and 74 Rue de Vaugirard. Today the site is in the city's bustling heart, and is home to the Catholic University of Paris. Anyone can walk in the gathered silence of the friar's monastery life by visiting what remains of it: the 1625 Saint Joseph Carmelite Church, crypt, corridors, cells, and garden area. This is where he for over fifty years grew his practice of the presence prayer.

Inside this Italian baroque building with dome, in his simple cell, in the garden, and in the kitchen, the friar built up a beautiful soul one ordinary attentive moment at a time. Beaufort reveals this in *The Profile*:

> Brother Lawrence began . . . by frequently cultivating in his heart this exalted awareness of God's presence, contemplated by faith. By continual acts of adoration, love, and requests for our Friend's help in what he had to do, he sustained this conversation. Then after completing a task he thanked God. . . . Since these spiritual acts were in this way connected with his daily tasks, and since his tasks provided material for these acts, he did his work more easily. Rather than diverting him from his work, his prayers helped him do it well.

NO SHOES, NO SATIN COAT

When in mid-August 1640 at the age of twenty-six Herman entered the monastery and took the religious name of Brother Lawrence of the Resurrection, he embraced owning nothing, not even a pair of proper shoes. Founders of the Discalced Carmelites, Teresa of Ávila (1515–1582) and John of the Cross (1542–1591), grounded this shoeless poverty in that of the Desert Mothers and Fathers. *Discalced*, pronounced with the second *c* soft like *s*, is Latin for "without [*dis-*] shoes [*calceus*]." A *calceus* was a close-toed leather boot, worn by Roman patricians, senators, and other powerful wealthy people. As a sign of the friar's vow of poverty, for fifty years Brother Lawrence wore sandals and a brown habit of undyed, rough wool.

We contrast this garb with the very different *habit habillé*, the multicolored, bejeweled satin coat worn in the Sun King's court, seventeen kilometers west in the same country, but in another world.

During Brother Lawrence's two-year novitiate, or monastic trial period, he adapted to the structure of a friar's life, aspiring to pray always and everywhere. He attended spiritual formation classes. And daily he observed communal prayer in the Liturgy of the Hours and Mass, and spent two hours in the silent med-itation or "mental prayer" (*oración mental*) that Teresa defined as a conversation with divine Love. He also had regular times for work/study, recreation, and community meetings.

BECOMING BROTHER LAWRENCE: FROM KITCHEN TO SANDAL SHOP

After the two years' novitiate, Brother Lawrence made his profes-sion of vows on August 14, 1642. He was twenty-eight. A decade had passed since his mystical experience with the leafless, lifeless tree in winter.

He dedicated himself to prayer and manual work. He accepted his place on the margins of the First Estate. As a mendicant friar (*mendicare* is Latin for "beg"), he was tasked with going out into the community to ask for alms for the monastery's living expenses. As a lay brother, he also had a minimal voice in monastic decision-making. He had duties that often kept him from the morning or evening hours of silent prayer that the other monks were given, and he was also called on to serve the priests' Masses in the morning.

Starting out a cook in training, young Brother Lawrence was later assigned as principal cook, preparing food for the hundred or so friars, following their dietary restrictions (for example, no meat). While he admitted hating kitchen work, he also found much material for soul work in it. For about fifteen years he was principal cook, a long time to do a job a person dislikes. If we count his time as cook in training, principal cook, and then as helper, he worked in the kitchen some forty years. Still, as Beaufort tells us, he did it "with the greatest love possible."

In that busy kitchen the friar's pain and God's grace meeting it organically is how his presence practice grew like dew, or mist on mountains. Before he made, say, a stew, he lifted his mind to Love, or asked for help to make a good meal for his brothers, or offered up his irritation for being assigned to the kitchen. Then when he stirred the stew he lifted his heart to the divine in thanks for the food, or perhaps in joy for a remembered blessing like a tree he'd walked past earlier in the day, and when the stew had been eaten, he thought with gratitude on its success, even as he knew with a sigh that the pots must be washed. We look for a method or a process, when prayer is simply intention in the middle of dirty dishes, and gratitude for a meal.

Then when Brother Lawrence was in his mid-forties, difficulties with his war-injured leg increased. His leg developed a large ulcer, and his monastery superiors assigned him to the sandal shop, or *savaterie*, where he could rest his leg, sitting more. His kitchen duties were reduced to peeling vegetables on feast days, and occasionally being sent out to buy wine. From then on, Brother Lawrence enjoyed repairing his Discalced Carmelite brothers' sandals.

His assignment to the monastery sandal shop brought him genuine "*délice*" or delight, as he told Beaufort in one conversation. Even so, he added that "he was ready to give up this job," because he could "find joy everywhere doing little things for the love of God." The sandal shop, Beaufort noted, best suited the friar's natural affinities for contemplation: "letting him cultivate—or perfect—a more mature awareness of God's presence."

In these ways, he gradually taught his mind, heart, soul, body, and self to love.

DECADES OF DISABILITY

Somehow the friar's practice of the presence prayer persisted even through chronic pain. At fifty-two, Brother Lawrence began having increasingly painful disability in his leg. This continued for the last twenty-five years of his life. When sent on one business trip to Burgundy by river, to buy wine for the monastery community, he experienced such limited mobility that he could "only move about on the boat by rolling himself over the barrels." The pain and issues with mobility progressed such that in the last two years of his life he was unable to walk.

Many have commented on the friar's wisdom related to human suffering. Archbishop Fénelon, visiting Brother Lawrence when the friar was ill, captured his calm spirit and lack of fear: "I went to see him when he was very sick yet very cheerful, and we had an excellent conversation about death," Fénelon wrote in his August 5, 1700, letter.

In the middle of pain Brother Lawrence discovered what spiritual teacher and scholar Barbara A. Holmes names "joy unspeakable" and he too calls "*contentemen[t]s indicibles*," trans-lated in his third conversation as "unspeakable joy." Holmes knows this joy unspeakable "is not silent," "is drum talk / that invites the spirits / to dance with us," "is respite / from the mad-dening crowds," "is that moment of / mystical encounter," and "is a symphony of incongruities / . . . and the wonder of surviving together." Reading *Joy Unspeakable*, her study of the contempla-tive tradition of the Black church, that inhabits "a vibrant and lived theology," with practices emanating from "soil, sun, life, and death," I was mindful that this is the spiritual wellspring for the friar's embodied prayer practice.

Through the rhythm of work and prayer, community and sol-itude, singing and silence, Brother Lawrence slowly lived into the healing practice of Presence during his difficult first monas-tic decade of spiritual and emotional struggle, and he gradually crafted and sustained an inner peace that lasted from thirty-six until his death at seventy-seven. He says that he practiced "a con-scious presence of God" that became "second nature" to him, and was his "soul's life and peace" for forty-plus years.

THE UNLIKELY FRIENDSHIP AT THE HEART OF THIS BOOK

For these insights into the friar's wisdom and life, we can thank his friend Joseph of Beaufort. A young Parisian priest when he first showed up to visit the former soldier from Lorraine turned cook and then monastery sandal maker, Beaufort saw Brother Lawrence as a spiritual mentor. Thankfully, he took many notes on their conversations. And after his friend's death, he also "care-fully gathered" what he could find that Brother Lawrence "him-self had written down," sixteen surviving *Letters*, and the *Spiritual Maxims*.

With these, Beaufort became the friar's initially anonymous biographer and publisher. In part it was an act of friendship. And convinced that the friar's writing was very "helpful, graceful, and welcoming," he and other friends of Brother Lawrence "didn't want to be the only ones benefiting," as Beaufort said.

You can generally tell a lot about somebody by looking at their friends. It makes sense that these two men bonded, though separated in age by a generation and by society's stratifications. Although Beaufort's father was a rich merchant who became the king's secretary, and Beaufort himself had status, he was self-effacing like his friend, preferring second place. Not until the 1710 third edition of *Practice of the Presence* did anyone discover Beaufort's name as the friar's biographer.

By the time Beaufort became vicar general of the bishop of Châlons-sur-Marne, he was also well-positioned to publish and defend his friend's writings, especially during the tense time of Christian infighting known as the Quietist controversy.

Out of the cruelty and catastrophe that racked the seventeenth century, a small, unlikely, and surprisingly sturdy book grew from a friendship and its conversations, to teach us about love in hard times.

HIS GOODNESS MADE HIM GENTLE

We have seen how the very human Nicolas Herman became the very calm, loving, and still very human Brother Lawrence of the Resurrection. By returning to micro-moments of loving conversation with the divine, never flawlessly but as best and as often as he could during each day, over the days, throughout decades, he grew in calmness and in presence. This practice changed him for the better. And he enjoyed life more.

The best description I know of him is, unsurprisingly, by his good friend and mentee Joseph of Beaufort. It's from the *Profile*:

The virtue of Brother Lawrence never made him harsh. His goodness made him gentle. He was a warm, welcoming person. He gave others confidence. When you met him, you felt you could tell him anything. You knew you'd found a friend. As for him, once he knew the person he was dealing with, he spoke freely and showed great kindness. He said simple things, but these were always to the point, and full of common sense and meaning. Once you got past his rough exterior, you discovered a unique wisdom, an openness of mind and a spaciousness beyond the reach of an ordinary lay brother. His depth of insight exceeded all expectation. . . . And you could consult him on anything.

On the pages that follow, you will meet this genuine soul who lives in these words. His authenticity flowed from his friendship with the Presence. His gentleness and warmth, great kindness and common sense, wisdom and openness of mind, which made him a wonderful friend, are the spiritual muscles that his practice of the presence prayer developed, over time.

Brother Lawrence is the reason this wise book has stayed alive through centuries of plague, famine, inequity, inhumanity, religious strife, wars, floods, and our ever-present human fragility. He extends friendship and wisdom to you.

Enjoy becoming friends, and spending time with him, returning now and again for conversation.

TRANSLATOR'S NOTE

A down-to-earth mystic, Brother Lawrence shares wisdom with a humble simplicity, of spirit and language, and my hope for this translation is to embody that.

It began silently. With doubts. Could I translate seventeenth-century French? A new challenge. I knew the friar first as fragments in articles and devotionals, and when asked years ago to write a piece on him, I'd only had time to read his work—well—in translation, so when I met him in the original and whole, would his words feed my soul? Would I find his theology genuinely kind? Would his teaching have practical application for my anxiety? In short, would his writings reward the kind of attention translation requires? So many unknowns.

I started by typing the friar's French words, letter by letter, directly reading from the 1692 first edition. And their meaning leapt from the page joyfully. And they *were* true. And they helped my soul immediately. Translating them was hard and yes I could do it, or rather, I was making progress, page after page of linguistic puzzles soothing me. Feeling his cheerful French words under my fingertips and hearing the rhythm of his calm voice and then revising the English translation one more time. By the end, my doubts had been alchemized into peace.

Each endless tiny effort made me happy, meditative, as a friend says knitting makes her feel. This intimate process is described vividly by Barthes translator Kate Briggs:

> I think we owe translators, and perhaps also ourselves, some recognition of what it might have meant *to have handled every single word* (space and punctuation mark) of the writing-to-be-translated, *to have taken a decision in relation to* its every single word (space and punctuation mark), . . . which might in turn be another way of saying *each and every one of its risks.*

Mindful that this singular experience almost defies description, Briggs essays anyway in *This Little Art*. And my translating experiences resonate with her musings on poet Paul Valéry's experiences translating Virgil from Latin to French, which he names a "making, unmaking, remaking, sacrificing here and there, restoring (as best I could) what I had first rejected." This "labor of approximation," as he called translation, "with its little successes, its regrets, its conquests, and its resignations" created in him "an interesting feeling (well known to me)," he says, of being "a poet at work."

What pulled me into Brother Lawrence's work and kept me there, bringing me back again and again, doing the re-seeing of revising, was his good heart. Where *good* means *kind.* Being with him is calming. Listen to these gentle lines that are the heart of his practice: "Above all, become accustomed to talking with God often. . . . We cannot put too much trust in such a good and faithful friend who will never let us down," words he wrote in his letters.

This loving, ordinary relationship is the practice of the presence. This simple prayer is a dynamic process that folds in kindness, conversation with the divine, and a constant state of return. It's a proven way to connect with our understanding of the numinous. His practice genuinely opens up to Mystery. And because of that, the practice of the presence transcends any boxing in of mystery and faith and community.

Brother Lawrence's teaching simplifies and deepens prayer and places prayer in the realm of mindfulness. The practice of the presence he says, is "the most sacred, the most robust, the easiest, and the most effective form of prayer." And even by wanting to practice it, we are already moving into Presence.

What also drew me to him was how real he is. He developed this practice from his own experience, a practice he needed for his own healing, and this translation honors and shares his personal wisdom. A disabled veteran living with a leg injury, a former prisoner of war, raised in poverty, lacking a traditional education, a Parisian with a tyrant for a king, a failed religious hermit, an ex-footman, a self-dubbed "clumsy oaf," a survivor of religious wars, a sufferer of anxiety, a man often in physical agony from war injuries, and a cook and sandal repairer, this lay brother regularly stopped work when chapel bells rang and headed to communal prayers, limping there, with red, still-wet dishpan hands.

His exceptional calm and responses to life's hardships make this unassuming friar an accessible and humanizing mentor of the time-tested practice of the presence prayer. *Practice of the Presence* offers new ways of seeing that surpass our sometimes tense and either-this-or-that mindsets. And my work with this translation seeks to honor and share his positive, open-hearted wisdom.

As a lover of words that do important, meaningful work, I respect, even love the pragmatic nature of the friar's teaching, which knows this practice as rising organically from human need, even as it helps those who read the words feel more at ease in their own skin. My intention, as congruent with the original writings of Brother Lawrence is to bring a translation that heals, making space for being happier and kinder. For those who engage in the process and the Presence, at first this will seem slow, but soon makes itself known as the most necessary, crafting deeply helpful changes to a soul.

This is practice that has been deeply personal for me. I know from my own experience of practicing it for decades in response to childhood trauma—before I even knew what Presence was, or that praying had begun. As I walked alone through endless sloping green pastures in rural red-earth Georgia, clambering over and sometimes snagging shorts on rusting sagging barbed-wire fences as a child and then as a teenager, I moved further into silence. Alongside grazing cows, white-gold oxeye daisies, and soaring red-tailed hawks as company, I experienced the way nature holds and teaches an injured soul, and understood that this prayer of Presence was somehow with me. Through good days, sad days, hard days, and thankful days, it continues, this familiar conversation.

Being-good-at-it is not the point, which makes the way of Brother Lawrence especially attractive. The friar invites us to contemplation that might begin with an injury, a joy, a job, a cup of coffee or tea, a new day, and/or any gritty, uncontrollable aspect of our human life. This practice turns to God or Love or however a person might conceive of Meaning, checks in, and comes back to the quotidian. This recursive process helps gently develop self-compassion, and also moves us into making a positive difference in our world. Many who practice this return to Presence, including me, find that when working with the mind like this, we might see needs arise as it brings up issues of trauma that want to be healed, so bringing in a spiritual director or therapist can be helpful for supporting the practice, and healing the wounds.

Because Brother Lawrence is practical, and teaches the universal theme of love, he has a following from diverse traditions that includes unaffiliated spiritual Nones, Roman Catholics and Protestants, meditation practitioners, Buddhists who appreciate his Zen approach, disciples of major religious groups, believers of other spiritual traditions, and those beyond conventional categories, including many not usually interested in religion or spirituality. Philosopher Aldous Huxley said the friar's practice of the presence "has enjoyed a kind of celebrity in circles otherwise completely uninterested in mental prayer or spiritual exercises."

My translation of *Practice of the Presence* walks out to meet this transboundary audience welcomed by the friar's wise teaching on Love. As I translated, I kept close to language that is current and timeless, I listened for English words with authenticity, accuracy, and inclusivity, and I opened for paradigm-shifts and relevance, because his teachings are relatable to a wide-ranging, global audience.

Translation is always with and always for. And as Brother Lawrence crossed the boundaries of time, reached beyond traditions, to Presence and to the persons around him, with love, this translation reaches widely as well, a translation that in the heart of Brother Lawrence is inclusive.

As I translated I was also teaching. And so my translating frame includes my students, who name themselves as African American, Asian, Asian American, Australian, Bahamian, Belarusian American, Black, British, Brown, Burmese, Cherokee, Chicanx, Chinese, Danish, Egyptian American, Ethiopian American, European, European American, Filipino American, Filipinx, German Italian American, Hmong, Honduran, Indigenous, Iranian, Israeli, Jamaican, Japanese American, Kenyan, Korean, Korean Polish Sicilian Hungarian American, Latina, Latine, Latino, Lebanese, Malaysian, Mestiza, Mexican, Mexican American, Native American, Navajo, Nawatl (Nahuatl), Nigerian, Norwegian, Polish, Romanian, Russian, Salvadoran, Senegalese, South Asian, South Korean, Sri Lankan, Swedish, Taiwanese, Turkish. They are diverse, and I seek to honor them by naming a few.

With this global audience in mind, I translated the friar's wisdom with respect for its original meaning in its early modern French and for its complex seventeenth-century historical context. My purpose in creating an accurate translation is crafted by my studies and years of teaching, publishing in linguistics, and experiences translating other spiritually profound works like *The Cloud of Unknowing*.

I also translated with respect for my experiences with self-compassion and with my neurodiverse mind. I translate with gratitude for patient K-12 educators who guided me when focusing seemed impossible because the alphabet was slippery, moving, swapping places, and I felt awkward, anxious, and afraid, believing I was a bad student then, while living for decades with an undiagnosed learning disability, dyslexia, and from age sixteen with untreated depression. Making long to-do lists and becoming high functioning, at a high personal cost. As a therapist told me: "You coped the best you could with what you knew then." Gradually, and partly because words stymied me, I became one of those studious, bespectacled people who loves etymologies. The heft of word histories was reassuring, because it provided ballast for floating letters, and helped me learn spellings and meanings. Also, because dyslexia meant that to read I had to look again and again at words, they became quite beautiful, the way you cannot stand on the rim of the Grand Canyon, look once, and see it all.

Re-seeing, it turns out, is what a translator needs. *Respect* "looks again," from the Latin *re-* "anew," and *specere* "look at," so respecting the text creates recursive processes that bring this translator joy. From the first day that I put my physical hands into the friar's French prose, typing his words directly from the first edition, feeling his rhythm and pulse, I revisited each word, often. *Respect* consults multiple dictionaries, reads history books, studies maps, searches older French works to meet words in their original contexts, and makes countless passes through a text. It rereads. It adjusts nuances. It starts over to do it again.

Respect's willingness to re-see nurtures *accuracy*, at heart a "doing with *care*, *caring*, taking *care* of," from the Latin *curare*, "cure, look after." One minor example of *accuracy* or *caring* was seeing a puzzling "*en soi*," "in itself" in modern French editions in contexts where it does not fit. So I looked again at the 1692 edition, and saw "*en foy*," "in faith" not "*en soi*." *Foy* was an alternative spelling of "*foi*" for "faith," which I translated. The friar uses "*foy*" intentionally, in word play, to communicate that the divine aid of "faith [*foy*]" empowers a person trying to practice the presence with "faithfulness [*fidélité*]." The stray "*soi*" happened when someone mistook the lowercased *f* in "*foy*" as a long *s* (ſ) (like a lowercased *f* with just a left-side nub), then changed the lettering to make the baffling "*soi*." "*En foi*" "in faith" appears multiple times in the friar's own writings. This translation brings *foy* back.

Proust and Flaubert translator Lydia Davis calls this approach of returning to a text "honoring it closely." You grow a translation.

As vital as accuracy for a translation is also joy. This is *joy* defined by cadence and by kindness. Reading the friar in French is beautiful and immersive, and the English sentences deserve a similar beauty, and sinew, rhythms and sounds enhancing meaning, drawing you back to hear them again, feel soothed, gain peace, and leave delighted.

Reading should also bring joy in the sense of inclusivity. New for translations of *Practice of the Presence* is this translation approach that honors its original welcoming spirit, which repeats "*tout le monde*" almost a dozen times, for "everybody or all," in communal senses like: we "all" share the experience of suffering, and we can "all" develop this mindful practice.

While Brother Lawrence—and mostly his editor Beaufort—lack the genderfluid approach to God of, say, a Julian of Norwich, the kindness practiced by the friar that drew Beaufort to him invited both to shake this off. As I revisited the text, the book's essence as wisdom literature, its Spirit, emerged, calling for freedom from a centuries-old prison of customary dualistic language.

Earlier translations sometimes even extended the convention of dualism by inserting masculine nouns and/or pronouns for French "*tous*" for "all [people]." Beaufort describes the friar's kindness in his eulogy: "He became everything to everyone [*tous*] to bring all to God," while traditional versions render it: "He became everything to all men [*tous*] to bring them all to God."

Also, feminine references in past translations were altered where the friar's original choices seem intentional. His "*maîtresse*," "mistress," in Letter 7 to a nun has in the past been translated as "master," even though this *maîtresse*, "mistress," shows his empathetic audience-focus in his letter to a nun who would appreciate his comparison to the balanced monastic power dynamic and to her woman-governed convent: "The will is the mistress of all our powers," as this translation reads.

Where the friar and priest use masculine images for God like "Lord, Master, King," "*Seigneur, Maître, Roi*," only some fifty times combined, this translation, reflecting on these words and their autocratic associations with seventeenth-century structures of inequity like feudalism and manorialism, consistently chooses "Friend, Teacher, Monarch" to represent the friar's healthy teaching for today. In such choices, this translation takes a text-aware, history-cognizant, wholistic, and community-minded approach that chimes with the friar's own teaching on Love.

This translation also honors and focuses on the trinitarian mystery integral to the friar's Carmelite spirituality and to his understanding of prayer. His trinitarian emphasis shows the influence of his spiritual ancestors. As Teresa of Ávila tells her convent sisters, "all three Persons" have "so much . . . mercy and kindness" that it is possible to experience this "divine company" in the "deep center of the soul," and John of the Cross teaches that the soul has a divine triune image and that God invites each to unite "in the Holy Trinity" in "power and wisdom and love." The friar shares their keen attention to participating daily in a loving, threefold deity.

This kind divine community of the Trinity woven throughout the friar's teaching is a bedrock reality of the Christian religion, a healthy threeness often missing or "remote" from everyday faith-life, as theologian Anne Hunt points out. Mystics like the friar, and thirteenth-century poet Mechthild of Magdeburg, however, express the mystery of the Trinity as their home, as Mechthild's personified Knowledge says to the Soul: "*Du bist dreifaltig in dir, / du kannst wohl Gottes Bild sein*," or "You yourself are threeness, / you can surely be God's image."

In this experience, God is three individuals who live in a community where difference is respected, and all are "radically equal and one," as Hunt notes. Trinitarian spirituality is "intensely relational," "inclusive of everyone and everything," and distinguished by "interdependence, charity, and love," again Hunt's words, and also a good summary of the friar's practice of the presence. To Brother Lawrence, the Trinity is the experience of friendship.

This binary-surpassing, unified threeness at the center of the lived spirituality of Brother Lawrence is one reason that the representation of God in this translation has a home in pronouns "they/themself/theirs." These signify the trinitarian mystery of Love, the friar's leitmotif, and limn the image of the Trinity's community, or *perichoresis*, described by Hunt as "the active, mutual, equal relations, without subordination" among God's three Persons, who are God the Parent, Jesus, and Spirit here.

These pronouns also respect the good kind news inherent in the *gospel*: *All are welcome*. When I read these words I can breathe.

And I hope they do the same for others, opening space for every person and for Mystery. Keeping in mind the friar's kind Trinity, and those marginalized by the power dynamic of the binary, this translation questions the philosophy underpinning the notion of translation purity in such a spiritual text, and gently moves beyond it, accurately.

As I translated and retranslated, and was myself translated, the gold dazzled in the work of this true mystic, whose wisdom asked me every day to keep an open mind. The translation's immediacy follows the approach of the friar.

My brief notes before each translated section frame the works. They give readers more background on his theology and use of language, insights into the friar's friends and others asking him for spiritual advice, where he was in his life's journey when he wrote the letters, and more on this book's rich publishing history. The appendices A, B, and C offer readers for the first time a timeline for the friar's life, eyewitness accounts of some of his century's catastrophes, and a schedule for how he spent his days. There are additional notes in the back matter. A Further Reading and Listening section provides more background materials, and updated links and resource materials can be found on my website at https://www.carmenbutcher.com/.

The book is organized so readers can start anywhere in the text. You don't have to go from start to finish. Dip in wherever you like. And may you find joy—and presence—here.

PRACTICE OF THE PRESENCE, THE TRANSLATION

NOTE TO THE READER

Although last year death took from us several Discalced Carmelites, both priests and lay brothers, who in dying left us rare examples of spiritual strengths, Providence seems to prefer that we focus our attention more on Brother Lawrence of the Resurrection than on the others.

Here is how Wisdom revealed this faithful friar's goodness. Throughout Brother Lawrence's life, he hid himself deliberately from others' view, and his goodness was not well recognized until his death. When a few spiritual people saw a copy of one of his letters and wanted to see more, we carefully gathered what we could find from what he himself had written down. Among these, we found a handwritten manuscript with the title *Spiritual Maxims, or Ways for Acquiring the Presence of God*.

These maxims and letters are so helpful, graceful, and welcoming, that those who felt encouraged by reading his works didn't want to be the only ones benefiting. They wanted these published. They wisely thought his writings would be very useful to souls seeking Love's perfection or wholeness by practicing the exercise of the presence of God taught here.

Since nothing is more persuasive for the practice of kindness than a good example, we decided that we would make this little work more complete by including a sketch of the author's life, where you see such a close connection between his actions and his words, that it becomes clear that Brother Lawrence very much spoke from his own experience.

Anyone seeking Love will find wise instruction here. Those busy in the world can see how misguided it is to look for peace and happiness in the empty spectacle of temporary things. The wise find encouraging teaching for persevering in the practice of compassion. Religious people, especially those not engaged in active ministry for the salvation of souls, can benefit especially, identifying here with one of our community. Like us, Brother Lawrence had many assigned duties, but in the middle of the most demanding jobs, he knew how to integrate action with contemplation so well that for more than forty years he almost never turned away from the presence of God, as you will see more fully in the rest of this book.

Joseph of Beaufort, editor
Paris
[1692]

1

SPIRITUAL MAXIMS

BY BROTHER LAWRENCE OF THE RESURRECTION

TRANSLATOR'S INTRODUCTION
TO THE *SPIRITUAL MAXIMS*

Brother Lawrence himself wrote down the *Spiritual Maxims*. Reading, we can almost hear the quiet of the monastery and the small scratching sound of his quill pen. This work presents his voice clearly, as also the *Letters* do. Beaufort says that this writing was discovered only after the friar's death when several people asked to see more of his letters. Gathering those, Beaufort found other handwritten sheets, the *Spiritual Maxims*.

The friar called it *Maximes spirituelles ou Moyens pour acquérir la présence de Dieu* (*Spiritual maxims, or the Ways to acquire the presence of God*). Since the word *maxim* is not in common use now, let's dust it off. Latin *maximus* means "greatest." In his day, as today, it meant "principle." When Brother Lawrence titled his thoughts *Spiritual Maxims*, he was simply saying: "Here are the essential points of my teaching on the practice of the presence."

The most essential point is love.

Brother Lawrence is the friar of *amour*. *Love* appears over one hundred times in the original text in diverse forms. After *love*, *grace* (*grâce*) is found almost eighty times, and *heart* (*cœur*) over sixty. These are three of his favorite words, showing up, combined, in what he himself penned, *Spiritual Maxims* and *Letters*, well over 100 times, and Beaufort follows his lead in his contributions to the book that mainly consist of selecting the friar's most important teachings, and recombining these.

In the friar's emphasis on *amour*, he brings to mind the fourteenth-century English mystic Julian of Norwich and her vision of the "kind Trinity," "*blissefull Trinite*," who "made all things for love." The first instance here uses the verb *aimer*, in the opening sentence: "Everything is possible . . . for those who *love* [*aime*]." An adverbial form comes soon after: "When we practice the presence, we enjoy . . . God's divine company, . . . looking to them *lovingly* [*amoureusement*] for support all the time."

The friar's maxims resonate with the ideas of Carmelite Teresa of Ávila. He promises that the practice of the presence helps a person "become familiar with" the divine presence, in Teresa's words "become accustomed to" or *acostumbrar*. We also find John of the Cross here, another root source in the friar's Carmelite tradition. When the friar describes the soul's actual union with God as "*un je ne sais quoi*," "an I don't know what" of the soul, he echoes the Spanish mystic's "*un no sé qué*" from his *Spiritual Canticle*.

As the modest friar often does, he refers to himself obliquely here: "I know someone who for forty years has been practicing a conscious presence of God." The "someone" is Brother Lawrence himself.

We also see that when discussing the esoteric three unions of the soul with God, the teacher-friar keeps it short and practical. In the French, these three unions are "*habituelle, virtuelle, actuelle*," "habitual, virtual, actual," in ascending order. I've kept these religious terms for consistency with the tradition of origin. The *virtual* doesn't mean "online" but rather comes from *virtue*, for "kindness," "goodness," and in the seventeenth century, also "strength, power."

This translation also embodies the inclusivity at the heart of the friar's triune, lived Carmelite faith, with "they/themself/

theirs," also "them/their," as the pronouns for God, as in the first maxim: "We always look to God and their kindness in all we do, say, and begin." As a reminder that this "their" refers to the Trinity, "the loving Three-in-One mystery" is included two sentences earlier.

SPIRITUAL MAXIMS

BY BROTHER LAWRENCE OF THE RESURRECTION

EVERYTHING IS POSSIBLE

Faith, hope & love

Everything is possible for those who believe, even more for those who hope, still more for those who love, and most of all for those who practice and persevere in these three powerful paths.

All who are baptized by true faith have taken the first step along the way of perfection, or union with the loving Three-in-One mystery. We will become perfect as long as we persevere in practicing the following maxims.

1. We always look to God and their kindness in all we do, say, and begin, since our purpose is to become the wisest lovers of God in this life, as we hope to be for all eternity. We firmly resolve to overcome with their grace all the difficulties found in the spiritual life.

2. When we take up the spiritual life, we need to think deeply about who we are. We will find ourselves deserving criticism, undeserving of the name *Christian*, and vulnerable to all sorts of problems and endless setbacks. These upset us and make our health, moods, affections, and outward behaviors

uneven. These show we are human, people God wants to teach humility through an endless number of internal and external troubles and anxieties.

3. We need to trust and not doubt that it is good for us and pleasing to God that we offer ourselves to Love. The ordinary course of God's divine providence allows us to experience all sorts of pain, troubles, and temptations, for the love of God, for as long as God wants. Without this submission of heart and mind to the will of Love, devotion and perfection—our pursuit of wholeness—cannot progress.

4. A soul depends on grace in proportion to its desire for a higher perfection, or completeness. God's help in every moment is even more necessary then, for without that grace the soul can do nothing. Obsession with worldly wealth, desire for power over those in our community, and a bedeviling preoccupation with others' opinions can together so fiercely and so relentlessly confront us, that without God's present help and this humble and necessary dependence, all these things would drag us away with them in spite of our resistance.

To our human nature, the practice of the presence seems hard, but grace likes it and rests there.

WORK GENTLY

1. The most sacred, most ordinary, and most necessary practice in the spiritual life is the presence of God. When we practice the presence, we enjoy and become familiar with God's divine company, speaking humbly and looking to them lovingly for support all the time, at every moment, without methods or limits, especially during times of temptation, pain, loneliness, exhaustion, and even disbelief and stumbling.

2. We will continually apply ourselves so that all our actions, without exception, become a kind of brief conversation with God, not self-consciously, but coming from the heart's goodness and simplicity.

3. We do all actions deliberately and thoughtfully, without being rash or rushed (which are signs of an untrained mind). We work gently and in love with God, asking them to accept our work. By our ongoing attention to God, we will break the cycle of harmfulness, and make all weapons fall.

4. During our work and other activities, even during our reading and writing, no matter how spiritual, and, I emphasize, even during our external devotions and vocal prayers, we must stop for a brief moment, as often as we can, to love God deep in our heart, to savor them, even though this is brief and in secret. Since you are aware that God is present before you during your actions, that they are in the deep center of your soul, why not stop your activities and even your vocal prayers, at least from time to time, to love God, praise them, ask for their help, offer them your heart, and thank them?

    What can please God more than if we leave all created things many times during the day to withdraw and respect Love present within? And this practice dissolves gradually, and almost unconsciously, the self-preoccupation that is such a part of human nature.

    Ultimately we can offer God no greater evidence of our faithfulness than by frequently detaching and turning from all things created so we can enjoy their Creator for a single moment. I don't mean to give the impression, though, that you should stop working or abandon your duties. That would be impossible. Wisdom, the mother of all our spiritual strengths, will be your guide. I am saying, however, that it is a common oversight among spiritually minded people not to turn from outside engagements from time to time to worship God within ourselves and enjoy in peace some small moments of their divine presence.

(This digression was long, but I thought the matter required all this explanation. Now let's get back to discussing our exercises.)

5. All this reverence must be done by faith, believing God is really living in our hearts, and we must honor, love, and serve them in spirit and in truth. God sees everything that happens and will happen in us and in all creatures, and Love is independent of all, the one on whom all creatures are depending, infinite in all kinds of perfections. Infinitely excellent and with sovereign power, they deserve all that we are, and everything in heaven and on earth, now and through eternity. All our thoughts, words, and actions belong rightly to God. Let's put this into practice.

6. We must carefully consider what qualities we most need to be kind. Which are the most difficult for us to develop, which ways of harming ourselves and others do we most often fall into, and which are the most frequent and predictable of our falls? At the moment of our struggle, we must turn back to God with complete confidence. Be still in the presence of divine majesty. Respect God humbly, telling them our heartaches and our weaknesses, and asking them lovingly for the help of their grace. This is how in our fragility we find in God our strength.

HUMBLE AND AUTHENTIC

How do we love God in spirit and in truth? This question presents three points for conversation.

I say, first, that loving God in spirit and in truth means loving God as we are created to love them. God is spirit, so we need to love them in spirit and in truth, that is, with a humble and authentic reverence of spirit in the deep center of our soul. Only

God can see this reverence. We can repeat it so often that it eventually becomes second nature to us, as if God is one with our soul, and our soul is one with God. Practice will make this clear.

Second, loving God in truth is recognizing God for what they are and recognizing ourselves for what we are. Loving God in truth is recognizing really, presently, and in spirit that God is what Love is, infinitely perfect, infinitely kind, infinitely far from all harming, and so on for every divine goodness. Who are we, and what reason could keep us from using every ounce of our strength to offer this amazing God all our respect and love?

Third, loving God in truth is admitting that our ways are completely contrary to Love's ways, and that God wants to make us like themself, if we want that. Who would be careless enough to turn away, even for a moment, from the respect, love, service, and constant thankfulness we owe God?

JE NE SAIS QUOI

Three kinds of spiritual union exist. The first is called habitual, the second is called virtual, and the third is called actual.

1. Habitual union is when we are united to God solely by Love's grace.
2. Virtual union is when we begin a kind action by which we are united to God and remain united with them by the strength of this action for as long as it continues.
3. Actual union is the most advanced. As it is completely spiritual, its movement is perceptible because the soul is not asleep as in the other unions, but finds herself powerfully stirred. Its activity is more intense than fire, and brighter than the sun when not obscured by cloud. We can, however, misunderstand this feeling, for it is not a simple expression of the heart, like saying, "My God, I love

you with all my heart," or other similar words. No, it is an *I don't know what*, a *je ne sais quoi* of the soul, a something indescribable, gentle, peaceful, spiritual, respectful, humble, loving, and very simple that carries the soul and nudges her to love, respect, and embrace God with a tenderness that cannot be expressed, and that only experience can conceive.

4.   All those who seek divine union need to know that anything that can delight the will in God is in fact agreeable and congenial to the union, or the will can make it so by way of inner joy.

   We need to admit that God is beyond our comprehension. To unite with them, we have to disengage our will from all sorts of spiritual and physical satisfactions, freeing us to love God above all things. If the will can in any way understand God, it can only be through love. A real difference exists between the will's preferences and feelings and its activities, because the will's preferences and feelings end in the soul, and its activity, which is truly love, ends in God, who has no boundary.

LIKE A STRAW FIRE

1.   The practice of the presence of God is an application of our mind to God. This reminder that God is present can be done either by the imagination or by the understanding.

2.   I know someone who for forty years has been practicing a conscious presence of God. He has several other names for this practice. Sometimes he calls it a simple act, or a clear and distinct experience of God. Other times, he says it is a blurry view or a general loving awareness of God, or a reminder of God. He also gives it names like attention to God, silent conversation with God, trust in God, or the soul's life and

peace. In essence, this person told me that all these phrases are merely synonyms for the same thing: the presence of God, a practice now second nature to him. Here is how.

3. He has formed this habit, he says, by acts of will that bring his mind back into God's presence frequently. So that as soon as he is free from his ordinary occupations—and often even when he is most engaged with these—the tip of his mind, the intent, or the highest part of his soul rises with no effort on his part, and remains as if it were suspended and fixed in God, above all earthly matters, finding its center and its place of rest. While held in this suspension he nearly always feels that faith accompanies his mind, so he is content. This is what he calls "actual presence of God," which includes all the other kinds of presence and much more besides, so that now he lives as if only God and he were in the world. He talks to God about everything, asking for what he needs, and being thankful with them constantly in countless ways.

4. But it's important to remember that this conversation with God takes place in the deep center of the soul. Here the soul speaks to God heart to heart, and always in an absolute and profound peace that the soul enjoys in God. Everything that takes place outside the soul is like a straw fire that goes out as soon as it ignites, and hardly ever, or very rarely, disturbs this inner peace.

5. To get back to the presence of God, let me say that this gentle, loving awareness of God lights a divine fire imperceptibly in the soul that glows so intensely with the love of God that we must do various activities to contain the external expression of these feelings.

6. We would surely be surprised if we knew what the soul sometimes says to God, who enjoys themself so much in these conversations that they allow the soul everything, providing the soul is willing to remain with God always, in the

soul's center. As if worried that the soul will return to created things, Love takes care to provide us with everything the soul can want. God does this so well that the soul often finds within itself a source of nourishment, very savory and delicious, even though the soul never knew it wanted this nourishment, did nothing to get it, and contributed nothing to it in any way, except by the soul's acceptance.

7.   That's how the presence of God is the soul's life and nourishment, acquired by Love's grace. Here are the ways:

HOW TO PRACTICE

1.   The first way to develop presence is in living each day with great simplicity.

2.   The second is in great faithfulness to the practice of this presence and to this inner awareness of God in faith, always gently, humbly, and lovingly doing this without giving in to hurry or anxiety.

3.   Taking special care that this inner awareness, no matter how brief, precedes our activities, that it accompanies these activities from time to time, and that we finish all tasks in the same way, we gradually grow the habit. Since this practice takes much time and effort to acquire, we must not get discouraged when we forget it, for any good habit is only formed with difficulty, but when it is formed, we will find contentment in all we do.

Isn't it fitting that the heart—first to pulse with life within us, and the part that controls the rest of the body—should be the first and the last to love and respect God, either by beginning or by finishing our spiritual and physical actions, and generally in all life's exercises? That is why the heart is where we must take care to produce this little inner look to God. We must do it simply and unselfconsciously, as I have said, to make it easier.

4. For those beginning this practice, forming a few words interiorly is helpful, like: "My God, I am all yours," or "God of love, I love you with all my heart," or "Love, create in me a new heart," or any other phrases love produces on the spot. Beginners must also however take care their minds do not wander, returning to the created universe and its creatures. If we keep the mind focused solely on God, it experiences being moved and led by the will, and the mind learns to be with God.

5. The practice of the presence of God, although a little difficult at first, secretly achieves marvelous effects in the soul, attracting an abundance of God's graces, and when done faithfully, it imperceptibly leads the soul to this simple awareness, to this loving view of God present everywhere. This is the most sacred, the most robust, the easiest, and the most effective form of prayer.

6. Please be aware that to arrive at this state requires our practice of self-control, since it is impossible for a soul to still indulge in worldly things and completely enjoy this divine presence. To be with God, we must let go of everything created.

This is how to practice the presence.

FAITH, HOPE, LOVE

1. The first benefit that the soul receives from the practice of the presence of God is that its faith becomes more alive and more active in all life's situations, especially where we most need it. This prayer easily finds grace for us in our temptations, and in our inevitable daily dealings with other people,

created and fallible just like us. In these moments the soul, accustomed to the practice of faith by this exercise, sees and senses God present by a simple remembering. The soul calls on God easily and effectively, receiving all it needs. In this way, we can say the soul experiences something very near the state of the blessed. The more the soul advances, the more its faith intensifies, and finally its faith becomes so vivid that you might even respond, saying: "I no longer believe, but I see and I experience."

2. The practice of the presence of God strengthens our hope. Our hope grows in proportion to our knowledge of Love. Through this sacred exercise our love increases as our faith experiences the secrets of the divinity. And our soul experiences a beauty infinitely beyond not only the physical bodies we see on earth, but even the beauty of the most loving souls and of angels. Our hope grows stronger and stronger as again and again we are calmed and sustained by the generosity of this Friendship we long for, and in some way already enjoy.

3. This practice inspires the will with a healthy skepticism of what it sees. And stirs within it the fire of sacred love. Since the will is always with God who is a powerful fire, this fire reduces to ashes all that is opposed to it. The soul, so stirred, can live only in the presence of God. This presence creates in the heart a healthy enthusiasm, a sacred listening, and a strong longing to see God loved, known, served, and respected by all creatures.

4. By turning inward with a glance to God and practicing the presence, through this returning awareness the soul becomes so familiar with divinity that the soul spends practically all its life in continual acts of love, reverence, contrition, trust, gratitude, giving, asking help, and all the best habits. Sometimes this prayer even develops into only one act that never

stops, because the soul constantly practices this exercise of God's divine presence.

I know that few people reach this degree of presence. The Trinity gives this grace solely to their closest friends, since this simple awareness is ultimately a gift from Love's kind hand. I will say, though, for the encouragement of those who want to embrace this holy practice, that God ordinarily gives it to souls willing to receive it. If God does not give it, we can at least acquire a way of praying and a state of prayer that—with the help of ordinary grace, and through this practice of the presence of God—come very close to this simple awareness.

2

LETTERS

BY BROTHER LAWRENCE OF THE RESURRECTION

LETTERS

BY FATHER LAWRENCE OF THE RESURRECTION

TRANSLATOR'S INTRODUCTION
TO THE *LETTERS*

These sixteen letters are what survive of likely many more written by Brother Lawrence. Spanning the last decade of his life, they represent his matured thinking and teaching. His friend and editor Joseph of Beaufort tells us how these came to be published. Although the friar "hid himself deliberately from others' view" while alive, a copy of one of his letters was read by several people, whether shared by Beaufort, or perhaps someone hadn't returned a copy loaned out earlier by the friar. These friends "wanted to see more," so Beaufort collected all that he could find of what his friend had written down.

The letters center on the practice of the presence of God—the friar's search for, struggles with, and joyful experience of this. Even so, their bassline is the theme of suffering. When he speaks here about dealing with pain, we remember that as a wounded veteran of the Thirty Years' War, Brother Lawrence lived for nearly fifty-five years with a painful disability in one leg, and that seventeenth-century medical help was limited to leeches and bloodletting. Dating from June 1, 1682, to six days before the friar died on February 12, 1691, the letters witness to how he handled his last hard days.

The friar's letters form brief conversations with his friends and others who write asking for his help. Mostly he writes to nuns, also to laywomen, and to one Carmelite friar or priest who is a spiritual director. Readers discover a curious "N—" in some of these. For privacy reasons, Beaufort replaced correspondents' names and others referenced here with "N—" for *Nom* or "Name."

This translation arranges the friar's letters chronologically, for ease of reading, using the Conrad de Meester *Critical Edition* and other research. The few letters without dates are pinpointed by textual clues, like a feast day reference. Because letters to repeat recipients are given successively here, readers have a continuous narrative of topics from letter to letter. You don't face gaps of comprehension when enjoying them.

The letters' simple salutations have been kept close to the original style. In these, the friar uses titles like "*Madame, Monsieur, Mademoiselle.*" To avoid such old-school greetings, in real life I use the correspondents' names. Since names were replaced by Beaufort with "N—," these appear in the text as "Madame of N—," "Mademoiselle of N—," and "Monsieur of N—" (sometimes without the "of"), keeping the French since it epitomizes the time period.

Each letter's title is a quote I've taken from the letter that focuses its message. Underneath titles, readers find the correspondent's vocation or position. A brief translator's note before each letter frames its specific significance.

LETTER 1 TRANSLATOR'S NOTE

SEE FOR YOURSELF

Brother Lawrence addresses this first letter to a nun, "*Ma Révérende Mère*," "Reverend Mother," who may have lived in one of the two convents built on the gardens on the north side of the monastery. The modest friar tries to erase himself from this text, where readers will notice throughout the letter that "he, him, his, himself" refer to "I, me, my, myself." He begins this way in the first sentence, where he refers to "one of our friars," who is himself.

At the time he wrote this letter he would have been sixty-eight or so. In it he explains that when he is "most engaged in his outward activities," he often feels "inner nudges" to bring himself back to the mindful practice of the presence. That observation conveys the information that, at nearly seventy, he is still physically active as the monastery sandal maker and as a kitchen helper.

We also see some of his signature, joyful word play here. Talking about himself, he writes: "If sometimes he is a little too forgetful [*absent*] of this divine presence [*présence*], God, the loving Trinity, immediately ... remind[s] him, calling him back." The French *absent* for "forgetful," from *ab-* "away from" and *esse* "be," meaning "not present with," is met in the clause by a reminder from *présence* or "being."

The friar adds that God gives "inner nudges" to remind him, "calling him back," or "*pour le rappeler*." His *rappeler* for "calling back" holds a universal falconry image that mystics often use to refer to spiritual transformation. *Rappel* means "to call a hawk back." Very like the gradual process of learning this spiritual practice, training a falcon takes time and patience. The falconer starts by attaching a leash to one of the bird's legs and letting it fly short distances, until it can be loosed to fly free and far, and yet trusted to return by simply being called back.

The inclusion of "the loving Trinity" here emphasizes the friar's mystical trinitarian Carmelite spirituality, which inspired "they/themself/theirs" as God's pronouns, and it also reminds readers that the "themself" in the sentence refers to God: "God, the loving Trinity, immediately makes themself felt in his soul to remind him, calling him back."

Again, the N— in the first sentence refers to a name Beaufort redacted for privacy.

LETTER 1

TO A NUN

SEE FOR YOURSELF

Reverend Mother,

I am taking this opportunity from N— to share with you the thoughts of one of our friars on the wonderful results and ongoing help he receives from practicing the presence of God. Let's benefit from these.

You'll see his main concern has been on being with God always. As a friar for over forty years, he's focused on doing, saying, and thinking only what pleases Love. Nothing else interests him, only the true love of God, who deserves infinitely more.

He is now so familiar with Love's divine presence that he receives constant help in every situation. For some thirty years his soul has experienced such continual and sometimes such intense inner joys that he must act in childish ways to contain all the joys and to keep these from showing outwardly. This behavior makes him feel more foolish than faithful.

If sometimes he is a little too forgetful of this divine presence, God, the loving Trinity, immediately makes themself felt in his soul to remind him, calling him back. This often happens when he is most engaged in his outward activities, and he responds very faithfully to these inner nudges. He will either lift his heart to God, or give them a soft and loving look, or say the words that love forms during these tête-à-têtes, like, "My God, I'm all yours. Friend, make me become your loving heart." Then he feels as if this God of love, content with these few words, falls back asleep and rests deep in the center of his soul. These experiences make him so certain that God is always in the depths of his soul, that he has no doubts about that, no matter what he's doing, and no matter what might happen to him.

You can see for yourself, Reverend Mother, how much contentment and satisfaction he enjoys. Constantly aware of such a rich treasure within himself, he has no anxiety about finding it. He doesn't suffer the pain of searching for it. It's completely accessible, and he's free to befriend mystery as he pleases.

He often mourns humanity's blindness. He cries out ceaselessly that we deserve compassion for settling for so little. "God," he says, "has infinite treasures to give us, but we're satisfied with some brief, tangible devotion. We are blind in this way, to tie God's hands and stop the abundance of Love's graces. But when God finds a soul filled with a living faith, they pour out graces in abundance. Then these flow like a strong river that, after being blocked from running its usual course, expands with power and abundance, when it finds release."

Yes, we often stop this powerful river by our lack of appreciation for it. Let's not stop it anymore, dear Mother. Let us return to ourselves. Break the dam, make way for grace, and mend the lost time. We may have little left to live. Death follows us closely, so let us be on guard. We only die once.

Again, we must return to ourselves. Time flies, and no escape. Everyone is accountable for herself, himself, or themself. I believe you have taken all necessary actions and will have no surprises. I praise you for that, for this is our work. Even so, we must keep on working, because in the spiritual life, not advancing is retreating. But those empowered by the breath of the holy Spirit sail on even when asleep. If the little ship of our soul is still rattled and tossed by winds or by storm, let's wake up the God who's resting there. Love will soon calm the sea.

I've taken the liberty, dearest Mother, to share such worthwhile experiences with you so you can compare these with your own. These can be useful in relighting and rekindling your own experiences, if—unfortunately, and God forbid, for it would be a tragedy—yours should ever cool down even slightly. Let us think back on the warmth we had when we began. Let us benefit from the example and experiences of this friar, little known in the world but known to God, and exquisitely caressed by them. I will request this grace for you. Very earnestly ask the same for the brother who is in our Friend,

Yours,

Brother Lawrence
From Paris
June 1, 1682

LETTER 2 TRANSLATOR'S NOTE

THE BREASTS OF GOD

Brother Lawrence writes this second and longest letter to "*Mon Révérende Père*," "Reverend Father," a spiritual director. In it he discusses the presence prayer as a "loving awareness" of divinity that brings rest at the very "center" of our being, which resonates with the teachings of the Discalced Carmelite founders, Teresa of Ávila and John of the Cross.

It also presents two of the friar's most profound images of divine love. In the first, he confesses being "guilty of committing all sorts of crimes" against his "Monarch," yet when he "declare[s] to God all the harm" he has "caused others" and asks for "Love's pardon," this "Ruler" does not punish him, but seats him before a meal and waits on him. The friar then moves intentionally from this forgiven criminal image to another memorable one that compares praying to the act of a baby nursing. He recalls Teresa of Ávila's description of her contemplative "prayer of quiet": "The soul is here like a baby at the breast." In prayer, Brother Lawrence says he experiences "unsayable sweetness," like an infant latched onto the "breast[s]" "*mamelles*" of a wet nurse.

Sometimes in traditional translations this image is omitted or euphemized, and "breasts of God" "*mamelles de Dieu*" rendered as "bosom of God." Because the friar's theology is embodied, *in a body*, lived, the more closely we look at this "*mamelles*" image, the more we understand his presence prayer. His *nourrice* for "wet nurse," often glossed as "mother," is a reminder of the economic disparity of his day. Wet nurses were in such demand by the aristocracy that twin terms existed: the *mère de lait*, milk mother, and the *mère de sang*, blood mother. Wet-nursing was a cottage industry, and we can wonder if young Nicolas Herman saw his mother wet-nursing babies, maybe sent out from Paris to stay a year in rural Hériménil, a custom that continued through the nineteenth century. Or perhaps Herman knew wet nurses who lived with the noble families he met while he was a footman for Monsieur of Fieubet.

Though this nursing image appears just once in his surviving writing, he likely used it more often, as identical language is found in the letters of the friar's informal student and high-ranking supporter, Archbishop François Fénelon. The archbishop studied, practiced, and shared the presence prayer with friends, and the friar's influence shows in his voluminous correspondence. Fénelon recommends the practice of the presence to a countess: "Take the nourishment God gives you; stay at the breast." A year later he writes, "Return to the breast of divine consolations." In another, he presents this prayer as nourishment: "Suck therefore the sweetest milk of love, from the breast of divine mercy. God gives you love, in the present time." Fénelon also describes practicing the presence as calming: "Keep in mind that silence, recollection, simplicity, and detachment from the world are for you what the breast of the wet nurse [*nourrice*] is for the infant."

In these letters, Archbishop Fénelon uses *mamelle* for "breast" and also *nourrice* for "nurse," similar to the friar. The choice of *nourrice* also contributes to the understanding of this prayer practice as wholly sustaining since *nourrice* shares with *nourishment* the Latin verb *nutrire* "to suckle."

Since the friar's theology, his way of knowing, does not separate the spiritual image from its physical truth, the more we ground our knowledge of this prayer in life's quotidian nature, the more we understand why it has endured and is so accessible. Anyone who has breastfed or supported someone who is breastfeeding knows the reality behind this beautiful image. Tired and sleep deprived, a woman finds lactating breasts are swollen, sometimes a baby has difficulties latching on for good suction, breast milk drips and trickles and has a faint and mildly sweet scent, and babies are not silent—but grunt, gulp, swallow; suck, swallow, breathe. A form of communication between mother and baby, breastfeeding can take some intimate learning, tummy to tummy in a snug fit. When the baby is latched on and the deeper rhythm happens with draw-swallow, the friar's "sweetness and pleasure" is a perfect phrasing. Then as the baby's stomach is nearing full and the baby becomes relaxed—no parent forgets the sweetness of a finally satiated baby, milk on the chin, asleep.

In this letter we hear the friar saying: As a baby is weak and needs total care, so the person practicing the presence prayer owns their weakness, opens to vulnerability, knows prayer as acceptance of hunger, and sucks for sustenance. It's messy. Anyone can do it who tries, and it is as familiar as the earliest days at the breast.

LETTER 2

TO A SPIRITUAL DIRECTOR

THE BREASTS OF GOD

Reverend Father,

I have not been able to find my way of life described in books, but this doesn't really bother me. I would, however, be very pleased to have the reassurance of knowing your thoughts on my present state.

A few days ago, in a conversation with a person of faith, I was told that the spiritual life is a life of grace that begins in abject fear, intensifies with the expectation of eternal life, and is consummated in pure love, and that each of these has different stages, through which we finally reach this blessed consummation.

I haven't followed these methods at all. Instead, and I don't know why, these scared me in the beginning. For this reason, when I entered religious life, I made a resolution to give myself entirely to God in atonement for my sins, and to renounce, for divine love, everything that was not God.

During the first years I usually filled set times of mental prayer with thoughts of death, judgment, hell, paradise, and my sins. I continued in this way for a few years, carefully applying myself the rest of the day, even while working, to practicing the presence of God, whom I always considered close to me, very often deep in my heart. This practice gave me such a high reverence for God, that in this matter faith was my sole reassurance.

Over time and without knowing it, I started doing the same thing during my set times of prayer, and this gave me great joy and comfort. This is how I began. I will admit that during the first ten years I suffered a great deal. My fear of not belonging to God as I wanted, my past sins always present before my eyes, and the amazing graces God gave me, these were the substance and source of all my sufferings. During this period I often fell, but I got back up immediately. I thought all creatures, reason, and even God themself were against me, and only faith was for me. Sometimes I was distressed by thoughts that this was the result of my presumption, that I had pretended to be suddenly where others arrive only with difficulty. Other times, I thought I was willingly damning myself, that there was no salvation for me.

When I accepted that I might spend the rest of my life suffering from these troubles and anxieties—which in no way diminished my trust in God, and only served to increase my faith—I found myself changed all at once. Then my soul, until that time always in unease, felt a deep inner peace as if finding the center and the place of rest.

From then on, I've done my work before God simply, in faith, with humility and love, and I give my whole self to doing, saying, and thinking only what might most please God. I hope that when I've done all I can, God will do with me as they please.

I cannot express to you what is happening in me at present. I feel no worry or doubt about my state since I have no other will than that of God, which I try to carry out in all things. I am so surrendered that I would not even pick up a straw from the ground against God's order, nor for any other reason than true love.

I gave up all devotions and prayers that are not required, and I focus only on being always in God's holy presence. I keep myself there by simple attentiveness and a general loving awareness of God. I could call this practicing the actual presence of God, or better, a silent and secret conversation of the soul with God that is lasting. This conversation sometimes gives me such great happiness and inner joys, and often even exterior ones, that to contain all that and prevent these from showing outwardly, I must do childish things that feel more foolish than faithful.

Finally, Reverend Father, I have no doubt that my soul has been with God for more than thirty years. I'm skipping over a lot of things in order not to bore you. I think it appropriate, however, to describe to you the way I see myself before God, whom I consider as my Sovereign.

I see myself as the most miserable of all human beings, stinking and covered in sores, guilty of committing all sorts of crimes against my Monarch. Moved by deep regret, I declare to God all the harm I have caused others. I ask Love's pardon. Then I give myself to their mercy to do with me as they please. Far from punishing me, this Ruler, full of kindness and mercy, lovingly embraces me, invites me to eat, seats me at Love's table, waits on me themself, gives me the keys to their treasures, and all in all, treats me like their favorite. My Sovereign talks with me and takes great pleasure in my company in countless ways, without ever mentioning my forgiveness or taking away my old habits. Although I beg Love to make me according to their heart, I always see myself as weaker and more miserable, and yet always more caressed by God. This is what I see from time to time while in God's holy presence.

My way is very ordinary. It is this simple attention, and this general loving awareness of God, where I often feel attached to sweetness and pleasure greater than an infant tastes when latched onto the breast of the wet nurse. So if I dared use this expression, I'd happily call this state the breasts of God, for the unsayable sweetness I taste and experience there.

If sometimes I turn away because of necessity or weakness, I am immediately called back by inner movements so charming and so delicious, that I'm embarrassed to speak of these. Please, Reverend Father, reflect on my great weaknesses, fully known to you, rather than on these great graces God kindly gives my soul, all unworthy and unknown as I am.

As for my set hours of prayer, these are now only a continuation of this same exercise. Sometimes I think of myself then as a stone in front of a sculptor who wants to carve a statue. Presenting myself in this way before God, I ask to be shaped in their loving image in my soul, making me completely like them.

At other times, as soon as I apply myself, I feel my whole mind and soul rise immediately, with no effort on my part, remaining suspended and immovably caught by God in my center, where I find my place of rest.

I understand some call this state idleness, self-deception, and self-absorption. I know from experience it is a sacred idleness, and a happy self-love, if the soul in this state could be capable of self-reflection. In fact, when the soul rests in this way, its former acts do not trouble it. In the past these habits supported the soul, but now would do more harm than good.

I cannot however allow this experience of God in my center to be called self-deception, since the soul who enjoys God there, only wants God. If this is self-deception in me, then it's up to God to remedy it. Let God do with me whatever they please. I want only God, and I want to be completely theirs.

Please write and let me know your opinion on this. It would mean a great deal to me, for I have a very special regard for your Reverence, and am, in our Friend,

Yours,

Brother Lawrence

LETTER 3 TRANSLATOR'S NOTE

START WHERE YOU ARE

In this third letter written to a nun, the friar addresses a Carmelite, likely a former convent leader, perhaps an ex-prioress. She may even be the "Carmelite nun" mentioned in *Last Words*. She also seems close in age to the friar, who was about seventy when he wrote this letter.

The exchange of books mentioned here suggests a closeness and community. "I will send you one of these books that discuss the practice of the presence of God," he writes to her. And in Letter 4 he follows up, a bit disappointed: "I'm surprised you haven't told me what you think of the book I sent you." While Letter 3 is undated, we know its earlier proximity to Letter 4, dated November 3, 1685.

A handful of the friar's surviving Letters, 3, 4, 5, 7, and 11, begin with the same salutation he uses here, "*Ma Révérende et Très Honorée Mère*," "Reverend and Very Honored Mother," and textual clues suggest that these plus Letter 8 were written to this same nun. Though Letter 8 has no salutation, Beaufort added "*à la même*," for its heading, suggesting it was sent "to the same" person as the previous letter.

In this letter, two of the friar's favorite adjectives for the practice of the presence prayer appear, when he tells her it is both "*nécessaire*" "necessary" and "*facile*" "easy." And his letter signs off with his oft-repeated, humble phrase: "I will help you with my prayers, poor [*pauvres*] as these are."

LETTER 3

TO A NUN

START WHERE YOU ARE

Reverend and Very Honored Mother,

Today I received two books and a letter from Sister N—. As she is preparing for her profession of vows, she asks for the prayers of your holy community, and for yours especially. She impresses me as having a remarkably strong confidence in your prayers, so don't disappoint her. Ask that she make her sacrifice only in the sight of God's love and with a firm resolve to be completely theirs.

I will send you one of these books about the practice of the presence of God. This is, in my opinion, the essence of all spiritual life, and it seems to me that by practicing it intentionally, you become spiritual in no time.

I know that to do this, the heart must be empty of all other things because God wants to enjoy it completely, and Love cannot enjoy it completely without emptying it of all that is not God, since without our full attention, God cannot act in it, or do in it what they please.

No way of life in this world is kinder or more gratifying than continual conversation with God. Only those who practice it and savor it can understand this. I do not suggest, however, that you do it for this reason. We must not be looking for consolations from this practice, but must do it from a motive of love and because God wants a loving approach.

If I were a preacher, I would preach nothing but the practice of the presence of God, and if I were a spiritual director, I would recommend it to everyone. I believe it's that necessary, and even easy.

Ah! If we only knew how much we need Love's graces and help, we would never lose sight of God, not even for a moment. Believe me. Make a sacred and intentional decision now, never to leave God willingly, and to live the rest of your life in this holy presence, even if for love of God, it meant to lose every consolation of heaven and earth, if God decides.

Put your hands to work. Start where you are. Do your best. Let this practice steady you, like an anchor, and you'll soon see the benefits. I will help you with my prayers, poor as these are. I commend myself earnestly to yours and to those of your holy community. My regards to all, and to you especially,

Your friend,

Brother Lawrence

LETTER 4 TRANSLATOR'S NOTE

BETTER LATE THAN NEVER

Addressed to the same "Reverend and Very Honored Mother" as the previous letter, Letter 4 was written on November 3, 1685. This seems to be one of six letters written to this same nun. The others are 3, 5, 7, 8, and 11.

The friar's letter comes with a sense of urgency for her to begin the motion of the heart: "Practice the presence diligently in your last days. Better late than never." In an indirect observation here, his choice of "religious people" seems to be directed to this nun: "I cannot understand how religious people can live content without the practice of the presence of God."

Even as he writes the letter with an urgency the previous letter doesn't have, he seems to understand that the "easy" task also comes with hurdles for others. He ends the letter by encouraging her to practice the presence prayer "despite all the difficulties."

LETTER 4

TO THE SAME NUN

BETTER LATE THAN NEVER

Reverend and Very Honored Mother,

I received from Mademoiselle of N— the rosaries you handed her to give to me. I'm surprised you haven't told me what you think of the book I sent you. You must have received it. Practice the presence diligently in your last days. Better late than never.

I cannot understand how religious people can live content without the practice of the presence of God. As for me, I withdraw with God and stay sheltered with Love deep in the center of my soul as much as I can. When I am with God in this way, I fear nothing, though the slightest turning away is hell for me.

This exercise does not hurt the body. It's a good idea, however, to deprive it occasionally, and even somewhat frequently, of several small, innocent, and acceptable pleasures. For God does not allow a soul who wants to be entirely theirs to have consolations other than with them. That's more than reasonable.

I'm not saying we must make our lives difficult while doing this, no. We serve God best in a sacred freedom. We work faithfully, without hurry or worry. Gently, calmly we bring our minds back to God, as many times as we find ourselves distracted.

We must put all our trust in God, though, and let go of all our cares. That includes letting go of a lot of private devotions, very good in themselves but often done for the wrong reasons. These are no more than means for arriving at an end. When through this exercise of the presence of God we are present with Love who is our end, then returning to the means is unnecessary.

Instead, we can continue our loving conversation with God, resting in the sacred presence, sometimes by an act of reverence, praise, or longing, other times by offering ourselves, thanksgiving, and anything else our minds can conceive.

Don't be discouraged by the opposition you feel from your human nature. You must exercise your will. In the beginning we may often think we're wasting our time, but we must continue, resolving to persevere until death, despite all the difficulties. I commend myself to the prayers of your holy community and to yours especially, and I am in our Friend,

Yours,

Brother Lawrence
From Paris on
November 3, 1685

LETTER 5 TRANSLATOR'S NOTE

I HOLD THEM CLOSE

Addressed to the "Reverend and Very Honored Mother," Letter 5 seems again to be one of six to the same nun, along with 3, 4, 7, 8, and 11. Brother Lawrence opens it by saying that his prayers for her, "though of little value," are "not in short supply," an ending similar to the close of Letter 3. Letter 5 has no date but fits well here based on clues in the content.

This letter indicates the influence of John of the Cross and Teresa of Ávila. Its emphasis on searching for wisdom's infinite treasures resonates with John's *Spiritual Canticle*, and the letter's benediction, "May they [God] be blessed by all" is often used by Teresa, including in her *Interior Castle*.

We find an edit in the middle of this letter. Beaufort excised a passage for reasons of privacy, inserting a note: "*[Brother Lawrence then talks about some private matters, before saying below:].*"

LETTER 5

TO THE SAME NUN

I HOLD THEM CLOSE

Reverend and Very Honored Mother,

My prayers, though of little value, are not in short supply. I promised to pray for you, and I keep my word. How happy we would be if we could only find the treasure talked about in the parables of Jesus. Everything else would seem like nothing to us. Since wisdom's treasures are infinite, the more we look and the deeper we dig, the more riches we find. Let's keep searching ceaselessly for it. Let's not get weary until we have found it.

[Brother Lawrence then talks about some private matters, before saying below:]

Finally, Reverend Mother, I do not know what will become of me. It seems that peace of mind and rest for my soul come to me even while I sleep. If I were capable of suffering, it would be from not having anything to suffer, and if I were permitted, I would willingly enter purgatory, where I believe I could suffer to atone for my sins, which would console me.

I only know that God looks after me. My tranquility is so complete that I fear nothing. What could I fear when I am with God? I hold them close with all I am. May they be blessed by all. *Amen.*

Yours,

Brother Lawrence

LETTER 6 TRANSLATOR'S NOTE

LITTLE BY LITTLE

This letter addressed to "*Madame*," a laywoman, is important for several reasons. It shows Brother Lawrence interacting with the community outside the cloister. When he recommends the practice of the presence to her friend who is a soldier, we remember the friar's own experience in the military in his youth and his injury in battle. We see him here as an encouraging teacher.

Dated October 12, 1688, Letter 6 is also significant because it comes near a turning point in the friar's life. From 1666 on, he'd had increasingly painful disability in his war-injured leg, pain that persisted through the last twenty-five years of his life. This disability progressed until he could not walk during his remaining two years, a period from about February 1, 1689, to his death on February 12, 1691. Letter 6 was written not long before he became unable to walk, with pain that must have been intense.

In the context of the friar's own struggles, his words of encouragement here seem profound. We see his empathy when he writes to this laywoman with advice for her soldier friend: "Let him remember to do this [prayer] whenever he can, and little by little he will get used to this simple but sacred practice."

The friar recommends that this correspondent's friend try doing the practice of the presence as a "brief awareness," an uncomplicated, repeated turning toward Love, "as often as possible." The essence of this prayer, as a "brief awareness," is common to mystic prayer. When the friar also describes it to this laywoman by saying that a "brief lifting up of the heart is enough," his words echo beyond Paris, across time and English Channel waters, and up past London to the East Midlands of England, where three centuries earlier a deliberately anonymous contemplative

I call Anonymous wrote the mysticism masterpiece *The Cloud of Unknowing*. The friar's "brief lifting up" is Anonymous's "*nakid entent*," a "simple reaching out, or stretching to God." Like Brother Lawrence, Anonymous reassures readers of the promise of the prayer: "You only need a naked intent for God. When you long for God, that's enough."

This naked intention, then, as with the friar's brief lifting up, is enough for us to receive the generosity of God's love.

LETTER 6

TO A LAYWOMAN

LITTLE BY LITTLE

Madame,

Our God is infinitely kind and knows what we need. I have always thought God would let you get to this point. Love will come to you in their time, and when you least expect it. Hope in God more than ever. Join me in being grateful for the graces given you, especially for the strength and patience God is giving you in your suffering. This is a clear sign that they care for you. Find comfort in God and thank them for everything.

I also admire the strength and courage of Monsieur of N—. God has given him a kind nature and a good will, but he is still a little worldly and very inexperienced. I hope the difficulty God sent him will be like a health-giving medicine, and will help him come to his senses. This is an opportunity for him to put all his trust in God who is always with him. May he think of God as often as he can, especially in times of greatest danger.

A brief lifting up of the heart is enough. A brief awareness of God, an inner act of affection—though running with sword in hand—these prayers, however short, are very pleasing to God, and far from causing those in battle to lose courage in the most dangerous situations, are strengthening.

Let him remember to do this whenever he can, and little by little he will get used to this simple but sacred practice. No one sees it, and nothing is easier than to repeat these brief inner acts of love frequently throughout the day. Please recommend that he remember God as often as possible in the way I've explained here.

This practice is very practical and necessary for a soldier exposed every day to threats to his life and often to his salvation. I hope God will help him and all the family, to whom I send greetings.

I am to all in general, and yours especially,

Your very humble friend,

Brother Lawrence
October 12, 1688

LETTER 7 TRANSLATOR'S NOTE

DON'T BE DISCOURAGED

We return in Letter 7 to the same nun who received Letters 3, 4, 5, 8, and 11. The friar wrote this in the time just before or as he became unable to walk. Though dateless, it fits well here based on content. Its theme explores how to handle distractions by practicing the presence. Brother Lawrence understood physical pain as a kind of distraction, and he discovered that this prayer practice creates rest for the mind, an experience of rest that he shares with his friend.

Centuries before the Internet, he reassures her: "You are telling me nothing new. . . . You're not the only one who has distracting thoughts." He explains the wandering mind as an absence of training: "When the mind has not been taught early on how to return, *to be led back* [*réduit*] to itself, it can develop some unhealthy habits of becoming distracted." *Réduit* for "*be led back*," found in English as *reduce*, means here that the distractible mind needs to be "*reduced*." This *réduit* is like the *reducing* that occurs from stirring a homemade spaghetti sauce all day until the arm feels a good soreness and the rich redness of the sauce deepens, spices open, and it *reduces* beautifully, condensing into a sweeter, tastier food. *Réduit* conveys his prayer's essential motion: "leading or bringing [*ducere*] back [*re-*]," where the *re-* expresses gentle, healthy repetition, a "going back . . . to the original place" of our truest self. Another meaning for *réduit* is "withdrawing to be restored," and in Cotgrave's 1611 dictionary: "conducted home againe."

The friar's instruction is especially relatable, as our minds crave this rest of being present, especially when distractions are not merely analog anymore, like a knock on the door, but are a constant rewiring of our brains via interfacing with computers, ubiquitous screens, and a 24/7/365 internet.

A thoughtful friend, a finance and law professional, texted me recently: "I struggle with the information age. . . . The ADD aspect of it & not pausing & being thoughtful are often too much." *Distraction*, like its word-relative *tractor*, has a "pulling" movement in it: the Latin root *trahere*, "to drag." *Distraction* is "a *being dragged* in different directions." When our humanity feels tenuous, we sense a need for sustained refocusing of our attention on Love. Brother Lawrence teaches the practice of the presence as a remedy for distraction.

He presents the prayer as a mindful "going back," a calm invisible stretching toward the source of selfhood. His favorite verb for the presence is *tenir*, for "hold or keep," from the ancient root **ten-* for "stretch." In this brief letter to his distracted friend, he repeats *tenir* four times: "*Hold* still before God," "*[K]eep* your mind in God's presence," "*[Keep] holding* it there," and "*Hold* it attentively in God's presence." This "holding" is not static, nor a numbed gripping. It is the soft stretching-toward someone that creates embrace. Practicing this, we notice that resting takes muscle too.

This **ten-* root appears in words that expand our understanding of ourselves and each other: a *tendon* "stretches," connects, keeps the body flexible, healthy; *tenderness* is "stretching" gently to be kind to someone; *attention* is "stretching" toward "*ad-*" someone to listen; and *contentment* is "stretching" together with "*con-*" someone or something loved.

Even the word *entretien*, the friar's oft-used word for "conversation," is a "stretching" between "*entre-*" two or more people, or as Cotgrave's 1611 dictionary has for the verb *entretenir*: "to *hold* in talke."

This prayer practice is a gentle soul stretching.

LETTER 7

TO A NUN

DON'T BE DISCOURAGED

Reverend and Very Honored Mother,

You are telling me nothing new in your letter. You're not the only one who has distracting thoughts. The mind is extremely likely to wander, but the will is the mistress of all our powers, and must draw the mind back and carry it to God as to its final end.

When the mind has not been taught early on how to return, to be led back to itself, it can develop some unhealthy habits of becoming distracted and scattered. These are difficult to over-come. These tendencies ordinarily drag us off to earthly things, in spite of ourselves.

I think that a solution for this is to admit our stumbles and humble ourselves before God. During set times of silent prayer, I advise you not to use many words. Long discourses often create distractions. Hold still before God in prayer like someone who is poor, who is unable to speak or walk, and who is waiting at the gate of a wealthy person. Do your best to keep your mind in God's presence. If it wanders or pulls away sometimes, don't be discouraged. Distress tends to distract the mind rather than to focus it. We must use the will gently to bring it back. If you persevere in this way, God will have mercy on you.

An easy way of bringing your mind back during the set time of prayer and holding it there more at rest, is not to let it wander much during the day. Hold it attentively in God's presence. As you get used to thinking of God from time to time, it will become easy to remain calm during times of prayer, or at least to bring the mind back when it wanders.

In my other letters I've already spoken at length with you about the benefits gained from this practice of the presence of God. Let's devote ourselves to it seriously and pray for each other. I commend myself to the prayers of Sister N— and of Reverend Mother N—, and am yours in our Friend,

Your very humble friend,

Brother Lawrence

LETTER 8 TRANSLATOR'S NOTE

SUDDENLY HOLY

By the time Brother Lawrence wrote this letter dated March 28, 1689, he was unable to walk. That difficult period began about February 1, 1689. As we read his last nine letters, we keep in mind that the friar was in his mid-to-late seventies, in acute chronic pain, and no longer independently mobile.

This letter also seems written to the nun who received Letters 3, 4, 5, 7, and 11. Its message fits well with the others often considered in this set. Though it has no salutation, Beaufort added "*à la même*" on it for "to the same," making it likely also addressed to "*Ma Révérende et Très Honorée Mère,*" "Reverend and Very Honored Mother" like the others. This greeting has been added here for consistency.

Even with the friar's challenges, his characteristic empathy shows when he writes, "You and I have spent more than forty years in religious life," since at this point, the friar had been in religious life about forty-nine years, but, as is his habit, he sees things from the perspective of the other person in the conversation.

He writes of the "parent of kindness," in the original as "*père de bonté,*" regularly rendered "Father of goodness," but *bonté* also referred to "kindness" in seventeenth-century usage. And this translation returns the term as consistent with the friar's cohesive teaching and language use on love.

Combined, the friar and the priest use the word *bonté* some sixteen times, and each one fits in context translated as "kindness," especially considering that the friar's spiritual experiences or lived theology rises above the traditional antagonistic discourse of dualisms of the time: sin versus holiness, sinner versus saint, wrong versus right, hell versus heaven, and badness versus goodness.

Liberating the original text's inherent "kindness" restores the friar's intent of facilitating Love's presence, moving beyond past translations that lean on dichotomies. This translation's beyond-dualistic view of life's biggest questions includes not only the friar's expansive use of *bonté*, but also his understanding of those terms like "evil," that others use for means of schism, where he might root that word instead in all that distracts us from God's presence. Brother Lawrence was ahead of his time in transcending either-or molds, and contemporary understandings on spiritual, emotional formation, and modern psychology have taken us beyond these groupings, helping us understand that dichotomies, and dualistic thinking, can injure our relationships, with our own self, with others, and with God.

The friar's (editor's, and/or printer's) use of capitalization around words relating to divinity tends to be somewhat haphazard. Here we see the lowercased "parent" referring to God, which recurs several times throughout the original French text. This letter does not capitalize pronouns for God, either, which suits my understanding of a nonhierarchical divinity, even as the French text mostly but not always uppercases metaphors for God. As long as the meaning has clarity, I usually follow its lead on that capitalization, as with "parent" here and "Parent" in Letter 12.

LETTER 8

TO THE SAME NUN

SUDDENLY HOLY

Reverend and Very Honored Mother,

Here is my reply to the letter I received from our dear Sister N—. Please take the trouble of giving it to her. Her heart seems to be in the right place, but she would like to go faster than grace. No one can be suddenly holy. I commend her to your care. We must help each other with our advice, and even more by our good examples. You'd be doing me a favor if you would let me know news of her from time to time, and if she is truly devoted and listening to the spirit.

We should often remember, dear Mother, that our only concern in this life is to please God. What can everything else be but nonsense and emptiness? You and I have spent more than forty years in religious life. Have we used these to love and serve God, whose mercy called us to do this? I am filled with shame and embarrassment when I reflect first on the abundant graces God has given me, and endlessly continues to give me, and then on my poor use of these, and my little progress along the way of perfection, which is the path of love.

Since God mercifully still gives us a little time, let's start right now. Let's make up for lost time. We can return with complete trust to this parent of kindness. They are always ready to receive us lovingly. Let's renounce, dear Mother, and freely give up for God's love all that is not God. They deserve infinitely more. Let us think of Love constantly. Let us put all our trust in them. I have no doubt that we will soon experience the benefits and know the abundance of Love's graces, with which we can do everything, and without which we can only do harm.

We cannot avoid the dangers and hazards that life is full of without God's actual, constant help. Let us ask them for it constantly. How can we ask for help unless we are with God? How can we be with God unless we think of them often? How can we think of them often unless we form a sacred habit of doing that?

You will tell me that I am always saying the same thing. It's true. I don't know of a better or easier way than this, and since I don't practice any other, I recommend it to everyone. We must become acquainted with a person before we can love them. To become acquainted with God, we must think of them often. Then when we love God, we will think of them very often, because our heart will be where our treasure is! Think about this often, and think about it carefully.

Your very humble friend,

Brother Lawrence
March 28, 1689

LETTER 9 TRANSLATOR'S NOTE

FAMILIAR CONVERSATIONS

In Letter 9, addressed to *"Madame,"* a laywoman "almost sixty-four," Brother Lawrence mentions his age, "I am nearly eighty," putting the undated letter likely at 1689. We remember that the friar at this time is no longer able to walk and is in significant daily pain.

In the words he writes, we hear the influence of Teresa of Ávila from *Way of Perfection*, when the friar describes how to practice the presence: "We don't need to shout out to do this. God is closer to us than we may think." Like Teresa, he also emphasizes that the practice of the presence of God is a habit that we "become accustomed to" (*"accoutumez vous"*). This phrase recurs in his writings, echoing her repetition of *acostumbrar* in the *Way of Perfection*, and elsewhere.

In this letter we see the friar reminding this laywoman that she can practice the presence at any time, "in the middle of your tasks." And he promises her that when she does, "the slightest little awareness will always be very pleasant." Also like Teresa, the friar teaches the presence prayer as a divine gift that also depends on human action, as he explains here: "Everyone is capable of these familiar conversations with God. . . . Let's begin."

LETTER 9

TO A LAYWOMAN

FAMILIAR CONVERSATIONS

Madame,

I feel very sorry for you. If you can leave your responsibilities with Monsieur and Madame N— and concern yourself only with praying to God, you would gain a huge victory. God does not ask much of us, merely a brief thought of them from time to time, a little love, sometimes asking for grace, sometimes offering them your sufferings, other times thanking them for the blessings they have given, and are giving you. In the middle of your tasks you can comfort yourself with Love as often as you can, in all these ways. During your meals and conversations, lift up your heart to God sometimes. The slightest little awareness will always be very pleasant. We don't need to shout out to do this. God is closer to us than we may think.

We don't always have to be in church to be with God. We can make our hearts an oratory where we withdraw from time to time to talk with them there, gently, humbly, and lovingly. Everyone is capable of these familiar conversations with God, some more, some less. Love knows what we can do. Let's begin. Perhaps God is only waiting for our kind intention.

Be brave. We have little time left to live. You are almost sixty-four, and I am nearly eighty. Let us live and die with God. Sufferings will always be gentle and agreeable to us when we are with God, and without God, the biggest pleasures are bitter agony. May God be thanked by all. *Amen.*

Gradually become accustomed to loving God in this way, asking for their grace, offering them your heart from time to time during the day, in the middle of your work, at any time you can. Don't stress yourself by adding special rules or private devotions. Do this in faith, with love and humility.

You can assure Monsieur and Madame of N— and Mademoiselle N— of my poor prayers, and that I am their servant, and especially yours in our Friend,

Yours,

Brother Lawrence

LETTER 10 TRANSLATOR'S NOTE

GOD DESIGNS HEARTS

Letter 10 is likely written to the same sixtysomething laywoman addressed in Letter 9: "*Madame*." Dated October 29, 1689, we know the friar wrote it during the hard last two years of his life, when he was unable to walk and experienced his worst daily pain.

One of the friar's favorite teaching points is that the mystery he calls "*Dieu*" is "a good and faithful friend who will never let us down." As a contemporary monk in Conyers, Georgia, once said to me, "God is our Friend. That's what most people need to know." As I listened to the monk, I understood I was one among those "most people." And here's how the friar puts that truth: "God is always near you and with you. Don't leave them alone. You would think it rude to leave a friend alone who came to visit you. Then why abandon God and leave them alone?"

As in his earlier Letter 6, likely to a different laywoman, the friar is once again asked to give advice to the correspondent's friend, who seems to have had some kind of relationship loss.

LETTER 10

TO THE SAME LAYWOMAN

GOD DESIGNS HEARTS

Madame,

I really had a lot of trouble getting myself to write to Monsieur of N—. I'm only doing it because you and Madame of N— requested this of me. Please take the trouble then of putting the address on it and making sure it gets to him.

I am very happy about the trust you have in God. May Love increase it in you more and more. We cannot put too much trust in such a good and faithful friend who will never let us down in this world or the next.

If Monsieur of N— can see how to benefit from the loss he has experienced, and if he puts all his trust in God, Love will soon give him another more powerful and better-intentioned friend. God designs hearts as they please. Perhaps there was too much worldliness and attachment to the friend he has lost. We must love our friends, but without forgetting the love of God which must come first.

Remember, I beg you, what I recommended. Think of God often, night and day, in all your activities, even when you relax. God is always near you and with you. Don't leave them alone. You would think it rude to leave a friend alone who came to visit you. Then why abandon God and leave them alone? Don't forget Love. Think of God often, and love them without stopping. Live and die with them. This is the beautiful work of those who follow the kind teachings of Jesus. In a word, it's our job. If we don't know it, we must learn it. I will help you with my prayers. I am in our Friend,

Yours,

Brother Lawrence
From Paris on
October 29, 1689

LETTER 11 TRANSLATOR'S NOTE

MY SOVEREIGN'S KINDNESS

This is the last of the surviving letters likely written to the same nun who was the recipient of Letters 3, 4, 5, 7, and 8. Again, she was likely a Carmelite and ex-prioress and a close contemporary of the friar. Perhaps she lived in one of the two convents behind the gardens of the monastery where the friar lived.

Thematically, you'll recall these letters are also interconnected in his emphasis that she practice the presence during her "troubles" and "suffering," as a remedy or "relief." When the friar discusses how to handle suffering here, he speaks from his experiences living with chronic pain and with disability in a day without advanced analgesics, antibiotics, or other scientific aids, and I am thankful for all these medical advancements, for scientists, and for dedicated, trained health-care professionals. When I read these passages, I appreciate their wise reminders to be humble, to turn to the mystery of Kindness and Power, and to listen to our holy bodies, our sacred selfhood, our self-worth, our wounds, our woundings, and our need for diverse healing, while I also see the friar writes from the location of his time, where medicines were often an endless search for a cure, and filled with poor science and often harmful results.

As we read this November 17, 1690, letter, we also remember that during the last two years of his life, he was unable to walk. Written three months before the death of Brother Lawrence, this letter also communicates that he is calm as well as aware that he is dying: "I will soon be going to see God," he writes.

The friar consistently presents his experience with divinity as one of repeated encounters with ultimate kindness. Like Letter 2,

Letter 11 includes the image of a forgiven criminal, communicating the friar's sense of being forgiven of his past. He writes to reassure his ailing friend of divine kindness, saying that although he sees himself as "the most notorious criminal in the world," he is still invited to "eat at the Monarch's table, and be served by their hands."

LETTER 11

TO A NUN

MY SOVEREIGN'S KINDNESS

Reverend and Very Honored Mother,

I don't ask God to deliver you from your troubles, but I do ask Love insistently that you be given the strength and patience to persist through these, as long as God wills. Calm yourself in the one who holds you, there at the cross. Love will release you when they consider it time. Happy are those who suffer with God. Become familiar with your suffering. Ask God for the strength to bear whatever they wish, and for as long as they think necessary. The world does not understand these truths, and I am not surprised. That's because some suffer as people of the world, not as those who follow Love. Some see illnesses as natural pains and not as graces from God, and from this perspective these people only encounter in suffering what thwarts and seems harsh to our human nature. But those who consider these as coming from the hand of God, as showing Love's mercy, and as a way of saving us and making us whole, ordinarily find in sufferings great gentleness and real comforts.

I wish I could convince you that God is often closer to us in times of illness and weakness than when we enjoy perfect health. In seeking to trust solely in medical remedies, often we forget to seek the doctor who is Love. As I understand it, Love always seeks a person's healing—body, soul, and will. Put your trust in them. By relying exclusively on medical remedies without also seeking the remedies of Love, we often delay our healing.

Healing ultimately comes from God, who permits medicines to work, who understands more deeply than we do, our cure. When suffering is allowed by God, only Love knows its cure. Seek love. Where God may allow us illnesses of the body we are to look also to the cure of the soul. Console yourself in the sovereign doctor of souls and bodies.

I can imagine your response. You'll tell me I have it easy since I eat and drink at Love's table. You are right. But do you think the suffering would be insignificant if the most notorious criminal in the world could eat at the Monarch's table, and be served by their hands, without being assured of their pardon? I believe he would feel such intense distress that only trust in his Sovereign's kindness could lessen it. Also, I can assure you, whatever delight I may feel in eating and drinking at my Monarch's table, my sins, always present before my eyes, and my doubts about my forgiveness, torment me, although, truth is, that suffering is agreeable to me.

Be content with the state in which God has placed you. No matter how happy you may think I am, I envy you. Pains and sufferings would be paradise for me if I could suffer with God, and the best pleasures would be hell, if I enjoyed these without God. All my consolation would be to suffer something for them.

I will soon be going to see God. I mean that I will go and give an account of my life. For if I can see God for a single moment, the sufferings of purgatory would be agreeable to me, even if these lasted until the end of the world. What comforts me in this life is that I see God by faith, and I see them in such a way that I can sometimes say, "I no longer believe, but I see. I experience what faith teaches us." With this assurance, and by this practice of faith, I will live and die with God.

Always keep God company. Love is the one and only relief for your troubles. I'll ask God to keep you company. My greetings to the Reverend Mother Prioress. I commend myself to her holy prayers, to the holy community's, to yours, and I am, in our Friend,

Yours,

Brother Lawrence
November 17, 1690

LETTER 12 TRANSLATOR'S NOTE

ALL FOR ALL

In the final months of his life, when he was unable to walk, and was aware he was dying, Brother Lawrence addressed Letter 12 to "Reverend Mother," likely the nun mentioned at the close of Letter 11 when he asked that "greetings" be given to the "Reverend Mother Prioress." Because of that possible link, and since Letter 12 has no date, it fits well after 11.

The letter starts out, "Since you insist," and then the friar kindly explains how he came to practicing the presence. After reading several books with different approaches of "going to God," he decided these would "only clutter" his mind "rather than make it easier" for him to find "a way of being completely with God." This experience caused him "to resolve to give all for all," which eventually led to the practice of "holding my mind in their holy presence, and calling my mind back to them as often as it was distracted."

As in the earlier Letters 2 and 11, the friar sees himself as a "criminal" who needs and receives God's forgiveness. Here he adds the image of himself as a child before God as his loving Parent: "I looked on Love in my heart as my Parent, as my God."

With this translation's focus on the message of radical forgiveness recurring in the friar's wise, psychologically healthy teaching, we remember that *péché* for "sin" and *mal* for "evil" appear only some thirty times in this entire book, with just a dozen of those uses by the friar, and with the other few by Beaufort. The friar's own language around "sin" and "evil" suggests the meaning of "causing harm" to someone else, and this harm always meets with forgiveness by a kind divine parent, who gently expects real changes in behavior and the making of amends.

The friar's writing echoes Teresa of Ávila again when he shares his initial struggles: "I had more than a few difficulties doing this exercise but continued despite these," words similar to hers in the *Way of Perfection*, where she states that beginnings can be hard: "at first it takes work [*trabajo*]."

LETTER 12

TO A NUN

ALL FOR ALL

Reverend Mother,

Since you insist, I will share with you the method I have used to arrive at this state of awareness of God's presence, where the mercy of our Friend has kindly put me. I cannot conceal from you how reluctantly I have been won over by your request. My condition in responding to it is that you don't show my letter to anyone. If I thought you would let anyone see it, even all my goodwill for your spiritual advancement could not compel me to write it.

So here is what I can tell you about it.

In several books I found different methods of going to God and various practices of the spiritual life. And these would—I believed—only clutter my mind rather than make it easier to find what I wanted. What I was seeking was nothing other than a way of being completely with God.

This led me to resolve to give all for all. Then after offering myself all to God to atone for my sins, for love of God I gave up everything that was not God, and I began to live as if only Love and I existed in the world. Sometimes I saw myself before God as a poor criminal at his Judge's feet, and at other times I looked on Love in my heart as my Parent, as my God. I loved them there as often as I could, holding my mind in their holy presence, and calling my mind back to them as often as it was distracted. I had more than a few difficulties doing this exercise but continued despite these, without getting worried or anxious when I was unintentionally distracted. I was as faithful to this practice during the day as I was during my set times of prayer, for at all times, at every hour, at every moment, even in the busiest times of my work, I banished and dismissed from my mind everything that could take the thought of God away from me.

This, Reverend Mother, has been my ordinary practice since I entered religious life. Although I've only practiced it in a weak and imperfect way, still I've received many profound benefits from it. I certainly know these blessings happened only through our Friend's mercy and kindness, since we can do nothing without them, and I even less so than everyone else. But when we faithfully stay in God's sacred presence, seeing them always before us, it not only helps us avoid upsetting or not pleasing Love—at least deliberately—but this awareness also helps us take the sacred liberty to ask them for the graces we need. Eventually, by repeating these acts, they become more familiar to us, and the presence of God becomes more natural. Join me in thanking them, please, for their great kindness to me. I can never thank God enough for the great number of graces they have given me, such a miserable sinner. May God be blessed by all. *Amen*. I am, in our Friend,

Yours,

Brother Lawrence

LETTERS 13–16 TRANSLATOR'S NOTES

THE EXERCISE, LOVE SOFTENS SUFFERING,
PEACE OF PARADISE, ONLY THE SWEETNESS

In this next set of letters written to his neighbor, we meet a nun who lived behind the friar's monastery in the Daughters of the Blessed Sacrament convent, which adjoined the monastery garden. This convent was founded in Lorraine in Rambervillers, which is twenty-nine kilometers south of his birthplace, and was also the site of the 1635 battle where the friar was wounded. During the Thirty Years' War, its nuns fled the Lorraine area in 1659 to settle in Paris. So she and Brother Lawrence may have shared a common background, and perhaps across the expanse of the garden a love for roses.

These four notes to this nun open with the most personal salutations of his surviving letters. We read, "*Ma Bonne Mère*," "Dear Mother" and "*Ma Très Chère Mère*," "Dearest Mother" or "Very Dear Mother." His comments within the letters suggest that this nun was very sick and had unsuccessfully sought help for her illness.

Facing his own pain, his inability to walk, and his nearing death, Brother Lawrence composed Letters 13–16 from a position alongside her in her suffering. For decades he'd lived with chronic and intensifying leg pain and disability, and within the severe limits of seventeenth-century medicine. In his passages on suffering, he tries to suggest that only seeking medical remedies won't lead to the cure, because love—through suffering—is pointing out that there isn't only bodily cure, but soul cure and will cure—and that Love has the insights to guide in all healing, but that also requires the person's surrender to Love.

In Letter 13 on November 28, 1690, he recommends the practice of the presence to his friend, as remedy: "If we were truly familiar with the exercise of the presence of God, all the illnesses of our bodies would become easy to bear." And when the friar writes, "Ask humbly and lovingly, as a child asks a kind parent, to resemble their sacred love," this translation reads inclusively for "*comme un enfant à son bon pére*": "as a child [asks] a kind parent," rather than a literal "as a child [asks] his good father."

In the opening of Letter 14 on December 21, 1690, we see the friar's empathy for this friend: "It hurts me to see you suffer for such a long time." And he reminds her: "Love softens suffering, and when we love God, we suffer for them with joy and courage. Do this, I beg you. Find comfort in God who is the one and only remedy for all our troubles."

As the friar of *amour*, Brother Lawrence finds his courage in love. In Letter 15, January 22, 1691, three weeks before he died, the seventy-seven-year-old dipped his goose-quill pen in oak-gall ink and wrote to this friend who experienced chronic pain: "*Prenez courage, ma très chère Mère,*" "Be brave, my very dear mother." It is touching that he sends her this cheer, for he himself lies in a bed of pain, dying. He encourages her to practice the presence: "If we want to enjoy the peace of paradise in this life, we must become accustomed to a familiar, humble, and loving conversation with God."

In his last letter, February 6, 1691, six days before his death, the friar tells her that when we look to God as to "a parent full of love," the "bitterness" of suffering "is removed." He assures her that "only the sweetness remains" then from "states of humiliation, pain, and suffering." He encourages her in his closing: "I cannot thank God enough for the little bit of relief you have received. I hope in Love's mercy for the grace of seeing God in a few days. Let us pray for each other."

Notably, he does not say "goodbye" or "*adieu*" in what he likely knew was his last letter to her. His use of the word *relief* in his closing would both comfort her, and refer her to helpful advice from his other letters; for example, to Letter 14, where he urges her to practice the presence of God: "Look for relief nowhere but in them." With these empathetic sentences, he puts a bookmark in their relationship, showing the nature of his empathy for others, his lack of fear when facing death, and his hope in a kind eternity.

LETTER 13

TO A NUN, A DAUGHTER OF THE BLESSED SACRAMENT

THE EXERCISE

Dear Mother,

If we were truly familiar with the exercise of the presence of God, all the illnesses of our bodies would become easy to bear. God often allows us to suffer some to refine our soul and to have us rest with them. I cannot understand how a soul who is with God, and wants only God, is capable of suffering. I have enough experience to be sure of this.

Have courage. Continually offer God your sorrows, and ask for strength to bear these. Above all, become accustomed to talking with God often. And try to forget them as little as possible. Love God even in your weaknesses, offering them your sufferings from time to time, even during your worst pain. Ask humbly and lovingly, as a child asks a kind parent, to resemble their sacred love, and to have the help of their grace. I will help you in this with my poor, small prayers.

God has many ways to draw us to themself. They sometimes hide from us. But faith—never lacking when needed—is our sole support, and the foundation of our trust, which we must put completely in God.

I do not know what God wants to do with me. I am always growing happier. Everyone suffers, and I, who should do rigorous penances, experience such ongoing and profound joys that I can scarcely contain these.

I would willingly ask God to let me share your sufferings, if I did not know my weakness, which is so great that if God left me alone for a moment, I'd be the most miserable of creatures. Yet I don't know how God could ever leave me alone, since faith lets me touch them. And they never pull away from us unless we pull away first.

Let's take care to stay near and not pull away from Love. Let's be with God always. Let's live and die with them. Pray to God for me, and I for you,

Your friend,

Brother Lawrence
November 28, 1690

LETTER 14

TO THE SAME NUN

LOVE SOFTENS SUFFERING

Dear Mother,

It hurts me to see you suffer for such a long time. What softens my sorrows for your pains is that I believe these show God's love for you. Look at all suffering this way, and you will find it easy to bear. My thought: Perhaps you've focused so entirely on human remedies that what's lost is a wider understanding of Love through the suffering? What if you surrender the driving desperation for human remedies only, and give yourself completely to divine Providence? Perhaps God is waiting for this yielding and for you to have total trust in them directing you to what truly will cure you. Since despite all your careful efforts these remedies have not had the expected effect, and instead the pain has increased, you can humbly give yourself into God's hands, and wait attentively on Love and Love's wisdom to heal.

Already in my last letter I told you that sometimes God may allow the body to suffer. When we are given suffering, that's when we cry out for a deeper cure, the cure for the disease of our souls. Be courageous. Turn your need into a strength. Ask God—not to be freed from the body's sorrows—but for the strength to be courageous, and suffer for their love whatever they wish, and for however long they wish. These prayers, though truly somewhat hard for our human nature, please God greatly, and comfort all who love them.

Love softens suffering, and when we love God, we suffer for them with joy and courage.

Do this, I beg you. Find comfort in God who is the one and only remedy for all our troubles. They are the parent of those in distress, always ready to come help us. God loves us infinitely more than we think. Love them, then. Look for relief nowhere but in them. I hope you will soon receive it.

Goodbye. I will help you with my prayers, poor as these are, and will always be in our Friend,

Yours,

Brother Lawrence
December 21, 1690

P.S. This morning, the feast of St. Thomas, I took Communion for you.

LETTER 15

TO THE SAME NUN

PEACE OF PARADISE

Dearest Mother,

I thank our Friend for lessening your pain some, as you hoped for. I have been near death many times. However, I've never felt so content as I did in those moments, so I did not ask for relief but for the strength to suffer courageously, humbly, and lovingly. Be brave, my very dear mother. Ah, how sweet and gentle it is to suffer with God. No matter how intense the pain is, accept it with love. Suffering becomes a paradise when we are with God. If we want to enjoy the peace of paradise in this life, we must become accustomed to a familiar, humble, and loving conversation with God.

We'll stop our minds from wandering away from God for any reason. We'll make our hearts a spiritual temple where we respect Love without ceasing. We'll look after ourselves with self-compassion, so we can learn to do, say, or think whatever most pleases God. When we're attentive to them in this way, suffering will no longer be anything but softness, balm, and consolation.

I know that to reach this state, the beginning is very difficult, and that we must act solely in faith. We also know that we can do all things with God's grace, and they never refuse anyone who asks them for it repeatedly. Knock on God's door, keep knocking, and I tell you that they will open to you in their time, if you don't get discouraged. Persevere, and Love will give you all at once what has been deferred for many years.

Goodbye. Pray for me, as I do for you. I hope to see God soon. I am all yours in our Friend,

Brother Lawrence
January 22, 1691

LETTER 16

TO THE SAME NUN

ONLY THE SWEETNESS

Dear Mother,

God knows very well what we need, and everything they do is for our good. If we knew how much they love us, we would always be ready to accept from their hand both the sweet and the bitter, and even the hardest and harshest things would be soft and gentle. Usually the most difficult sufferings seem unbearable only because of the way we look at these. When we are convinced the hand of God is at work in us, and that a parent full of love allows us to experience these states of humiliation, pain, and suffering, then all the bitterness is removed, and only the sweetness remains.

Let us devote ourselves entirely to knowing God as our Friend. The more we know them, the more we want to know them. Since love is ordinarily measured by how well we know someone, the deeper and more inclusive the knowing, the greater the love will be. And if our love is great, we will love God equally in pain and in joy.

Let us not stop short by seeking or loving God only for the graces they have given us or can give us, no matter how great these may be. All gifts, though impressive, never bring us as close to Love as does one simple act of faith. Let us seek God often through faith. Since God is within us, let's not look for them anywhere else. Aren't we being rude, and even guilty of leaving them alone, when we busy ourselves with so many unimportant things that don't please Love and might upset them? God puts up with these patiently, but we are wise to worry that one day our distractions may cost us dearly.

Let us begin to belong all to Love. Let's banish from our heart and mind all that is not love. God wants to be there solely, so let's ask for this grace. If we ourselves do what we can, we will soon see the change that we hope for in ourselves.

I cannot thank God enough for the little bit of relief you have received. I hope in Love's mercy for the grace of seeing God in a few days. Let us pray for each other. I am in our Friend,

Yours,

Brother Lawrence
February 6, 1691

On February 12, 1691, Brother Lawrence died, six days after writing this letter.

3

CONVERSATIONS
WITH BROTHER LAWRENCE

RECORDED BY JOSEPH OF BEAUFORT

TRANSLATOR'S INTRODUCTION
TO THE *CONVERSATIONS*

On August 3, 1666, a thirtysomething, well-educated priest, Joseph of Beaufort, began visiting with an uneducated, fifty-something friar, monastery sandal maker, and Thirty Years' War veteran, Brother Lawrence. On that Tuesday in Paris, Beaufort sought out this lay brother, considering him a *starets,* a spiritual father who could teach him wisdom. Their dialogue forms this book's foundation. Their conversations draw us into the heart of the friar's spirituality of love and community. Their shared stories give readers a concrete sense of the friar's humanity. Within these exchanges we meet a simple mystic.

After each of their first four conversations, the young Beaufort wrote down notes he recalled. Their talks occurred at the monastery over two autumns: August 3, September 28, and November 22, 1666, and November 25, 1667. In addition to repairing sandals, the friar was tasked with purchasing wine for the brothers, traveling by river six hundred kilometers to Burgundy to make the purchase. He also helped in the kitchen, though no longer as principal cook. That year—1666—his war-wounded leg worsened, and he would go on to live in intense pain the last twenty-five years of his life. The war injury took place in 1635, near the time of Beaufort's birth.

These *Conversations* were not included by Beaufort in part 1 of the first edition of *Practice of the Presence*. At the time—from 1690 on—he was vicar general, and perhaps Beaufort was so busy that he couldn't find all his notes. Luckily, eventually he found these, and published *Conversations* in part 2 of the first edition. Numbered and dated in the original, each conversation is also titled here with a quote from its text that highlights its essence.

Throughout the *Conversations* readers also find echoes of Teresa of Ávila, whose work was read aloud to the brothers during meals. Brother Lawrence says in the Fourth Conversation: "Don't get tired of doing little things for the love of God. They consider not the importance of the work but the love," resonating with *Interior Castle*: "[God] doesn't look at the greatness of your works but at the love with which these are done."

Composed from the firsthand notes of Beaufort, who must have been a good listener and a conscientious notetaker, *Conversations* lets us hear the voice of Brother Lawrence clearly. The vicar general himself best introduces these conversations in the *Profile*:

> Brother Lawrence will speak for himself. I will give you his own words taken from the conversations I had with him, which as soon as I left him I wrote down. No one can portray true people of faith better than these individuals, themselves. St. Augustine's *Confessions* and his *Letters* give us a much more authentic portrait than anything that could be said about him. In the same way, hearing what our friar himself said from the simplicity of his heart brings you closest to this friend of God. Nothing I could say could better help you see his spiritual strengths.

STRANGE GIFT

FIRST CONVERSATION

AUGUST 3, 1666

I went to see Brother Lawrence for the first time today. He told me that God had given him a strange and wonderful gift through his conversion, which occurred when he was eighteen and still "in the world." This happened before he entered the monastery. One day in winter as he was looking at a barren tree, stripped of its leaves, and considering how in a little while these leaves would reappear, green, followed by flowers and fruits, he received a profound awareness of God's kindness and power that never left his soul since. With this awareness he completely detached himself from the world, and it gave him such a love for God that he could not say it had ever increased during the more than forty years since he received this gift.

He continued, telling me that he had worked as the footman of Monsieur of Fieubet, the royal treasurer of savings, and was a clumsy oaf who broke everything.

After that time, he asked to enter a religious order. He thought he'd be skinned alive there for his clumsiness and shortcomings, even as through these he would be able to offer his life and all its pleasures to God. However, God fooled him, because the friar only experienced satisfaction. This often made him say, "You tricked me!" to God.

Brother Lawrence said that we must ground ourselves in God's presence by continually conversing with Love, and that it's a shame to leave this conversation with our divine Friend for thoughts that are sarcastic or shallow. We can nourish our soul best with a high consideration of God, the loving Trinity, which is how we draw great joy from being with them.

We must animate our faith. He said it's a pity that we have so little. Instead of taking faith as our guide for living, we busy ourselves with small devotions that vary every day. This way of faith is the spirit, heart, and mind of the community of Love's friends. And it's all we need to flourish and arrive at a high level of loving awareness.

If we give our self to God completely and generously in day-to-day matters and in spiritual ones, we will find our joy in carrying out Love's intentions, whether they lead us by the way of suffering or consolation. It's all the same when a person is really surrendered. We need faithfulness even in a dry period when it is hard to pray. God tests our love then, and when we make wise acts of giving in and yielding, we often find just one of these takes us a long way down the path.

As for the suffering and injustices that the friar hears about from those around him every day, these don't shock him; instead, he's surprised there aren't more injustices, considering the harm humans are capable of doing to each other. Brother Lawrence prays for those who cause harm. But knowing that God can at any time mend anyone, then he doesn't worry anymore about it.

To experience the freedom of the self in Love, as God wishes, we must study attentively all the movements our soul makes, both in spiritual matters as well as in the most common ones. God gives light for that to those who have a true longing to be with them. If that is my intention, the friar said, I can ask to see him whenever I want without fear of bothering him, and if not, I shouldn't come to see him at all.

SURPRISE OF WONDER

SECOND CONVERSATION

SEPTEMBER 28, 1666

Brother Lawrence said he always had been led by love. He let no other interest influence his way of living, and he never worried if he would be damned or saved. After he decided to do every action for the love of God, he experienced peace. He was content even with picking up a straw from the ground for the love of God, simply seeking just God, and nothing else, not even Love's gifts.

Responding to these attitudes and habits of the friar's soul, God gives him infinite graces, he said. Though we are free to accept the fruit of these graces—the love awakened—we must reject the taste, which is not God, since we know by faith that God is infinitely greater and completely other than what we feel about them. This understanding, he said, brings about a marvelous struggle between God and the soul: God gives, and the soul denies that what it receives is God. In this struggle, the soul is as strong in faith, and even stronger than God, since God can never give so much that the soul cannot always protest, saying that God is not what God gives, since Love is always greater than Love's gifts.

Ecstasy and unusual spiritual experiences are only encountered by a soul focusing on the gift, rather than rejecting the gift—and going beyond it—to God. Except for feeling the surprise of wonder, we shouldn't let ourselves get carried away. We bring our attention back to rest on God our teacher.

God rewards so promptly and so generously everything we do for them that Brother Lawrence sometimes wished he could hide from God what he was doing for love of them so that, by not receiving a reward, he could have the pleasure of doing something simply for Love.

He also shared that at one period of his life his spirit had been very distressed. He thought for certain he was damned. No one in the world could have convinced him otherwise. Eventually, however, he came to this conclusion: "I entered religious life only for the love of God. I've tried to act only for Love. Whether damned or saved, I always want to continue to act purely for the love of God. At least I'll have that in my favor. Until I die, I will do what is in me to love God." For four very painful years this anxiety followed him.

Since then, he thought neither about heaven nor about hell. His life was only inner freedom and constant joy. He placed his sins between God and himself, as if to remind God that he didn't deserve Love's graces. But that didn't stop God from filling him with blessings. He felt like God sometimes took him by the hand and presented him before the entire celestial court, showing off this distressed, needy soul to whom Love happily grants their abundant graces.

At first, when we're beginning to form the habit of conversing continually with God, we must somewhat apply ourselves to this practice, bringing everything we do back to Love, but after a little effort, we feel awakened by God's love without any difficulty.

The friar fully expected that after the good times God had given him, he would have his share of difficulties and pains. He didn't worry about it, though. He knew very well that since he could do nothing by himself, God would not forget to give him the strength to bear sufferings.

When presented with the opportunity to practice some act of kindness or patience, he always addressed himself to God, saying to them: "My God, I can only do this if you help me." And he received the strength he needed immediately, and more.

When Brother Lawrence fell short, or when he got distracted, he did nothing except acknowledge his lapse, saying to God: "I'll never do anything different if you leave me alone. It's up to you to stop me from stumbling and to mend what's wounded." After that, he didn't worry about his weakness.

He said we must act very simply with God, and talk to Love freely, asking them for help with things as life happens. And as he'd often experienced, God will never forget to give us help.

A few days ago he was told to go to Burgundy to buy the community's wine supply. This task proved painful and difficult for him not only because he had no business skills, he said, but also because he lived with the disability of an injured leg. He could only move about on the boat by rolling himself over the barrels. He didn't worry about that, however, any more than he did about the purchase of the wine. He told God it was their problem. After that, he found that all was done, and done well. He had been sent to Auvergne the previous year for the same reason. He couldn't say how this work had gotten done a year earlier, either, since he was also not the one who made it happen then, and yet it was done, and very well.

The same thing was true in the kitchen. Even though he had the strongest natural aversion to doing kitchen work, he grew accustomed to doing everything there for the love of God, asking in every situation for the grace to do this work. In this way he found his fifteen years there very easy.

More recently he was assigned to the sandal repair shop, which he enjoyed, but he said he was ready to give up this job, as he had the others. He was able to find joy everywhere doing little things for the love of God.

He said set times for the mental prayer of his Carmelite tradition were no different for him than other times. He retreated to pray when the Father Prior told him to, but he did not desire or ask for periods of prayer, since even his busiest, most demanding work didn't turn him away from God.

Knowing that it's necessary to love God in all things, and working to carry out this duty, he didn't seek a spiritual director but rather a confessor to receive absolution for his shortcomings and stumblings. He was well aware of—and not at all surprised by—his weaknesses. He confessed these to God and did not plead with God to excuse any. After that he returned in peace to his ordinary exercises of love and gratitude.

In his troubles he consulted no one. With the light of faith, knowing only that God was present, he was satisfied to act for Love, *come what may*. In this way he was willing to lose himself for the love of God, where he had found his soul, and was content.

Overthinking ruins everything. Our trouble starts in our thoughts, he said. We must be careful to reject these as soon as we notice our thinking has nothing to do with our present tasks or our well-being. Our good is found when we resume our conversation with God.

In the beginning, he would often spend the entire time set aside for prayer rejecting thoughts and then tumbling back into these same thoughts. Never was he able to pray by the rules like others. He did try in the beginning to meditate discursively for a while, but afterward he didn't know where the time and efforts had gone, and it would be impossible for him to explain even what had happened within it.

He asked his superiors at the monastery to remain forever a novice, not believing that anyone would find him fit to take his monastic vows, and hardly believing when the time came that the two years of his novitiate had passed.

He was not bold enough to ask God for penances. And he didn't really want to do any, even as he knew well that he deserved many. When God sent such to him, he knew Love would give him the grace to carry these out.

All penances and other exercises, he said, are designed only to facilitate union with God by love. After considering the purpose of all these carefully, he found it even shorter to go straight to union with God by a continual practice of love, by doing everything for the love of God.

There's a very distinct difference between the activities of the mind and those of the will. Our thoughts amount to little when compared with everything our will does. Loving and thanking God matter most.

Even if we could do all possible penances, if done without love, these would not help atone for a single harm we've caused. Without worrying, we must look for forgiveness by the blood of Jesus, working solely at loving God with all our heart. God seems to choose the worst sinners to give the greatest graces, rather than those who keep their innocence—because greater graces show God's kindness more.

He didn't think about death, his sins, paradise, or hell. He only thought of doing little things for the love of God, since he did not consider himself capable of doing great things. Then come what may, whatever happened to him was up to God, and he was at peace with that.

To be skinned alive would be nothing compared to the inner suffering he had experienced. Nor could it compare in intensity to the profound joys he'd often experienced and was still experiencing. That's why nothing worried him and nothing frightened him. He asked God only that he be kept from upsetting Love.

He told me that he rarely frets about the past: "When I know I've fallen short or been distracted, I accept it, saying: *That's typical for me. It's all I can do.* If I have not disappointed or been inattentive, but instead have done well, I thank God for it, and confess that this grace comes from them."

LOVING PRESENCE

THIRD CONVERSATION

NOVEMBER 22, 1666

Brother Lawrence told me that the ground of his spiritual life was a profound awareness and reverence for God made possible through faith. In the beginning, once awareness and reverence had taken root, his only concern was to faithfully reject every thought that was not God-toward, and to do all his actions for the love of God. Sometimes he went a long time without thinking about God, but he didn't let that trouble him. After he admitted his weakness or distress to God, he returned to them with more trust, and with a degree of confidence equal to the earlier regret he felt for forgetting Love.

The trust we have in God honors them greatly and brings us great graces.

God cannot deceive. It's also impossible for Love to let a soul suffer a long time, when that person is completely open with God and resolves to endure all for them.

Brother Lawrence reached the point where his thoughts were only of God. In his struggle with temptation—if he felt tempted to idolize someone else, or had some other temptation—he could sense these thoughts coming. But the experience he had of God's prompt help was so real that sometimes he let the thoughts advance. Then at just the right moment, he spoke to God, and these thoughts vanished instantly.

Similarly, when he had any external business to take care of, he did not think about it in advance. When the time came for action, he found in God, as in a clear mirror, what he needed to do in that present moment. For some now time now he acted in this way without worrying beforehand. Before this experience of God's prompt help with his tasks, however, he'd thought and worried about every single thing ahead of time.

When he accomplished his duties in God, he did not remember the things he did, and was hardly even aware of his tasks as he was doing these. When he left the table, he didn't know what he had eaten. He acted from the simplicity of his purpose, doing everything for the love of God. He gave thanks to God for directing his projects and countless other activities. All of these he also did very simply, in a way that held him rooted in the loving presence of God.

When any task somehow distracted him from thinking of God, a memory from God would move in his soul, enveloping him, giving him such an intense, warm awareness of Love, and stirring his love so strongly, that he cried out and moved away from distraction with great energy, singing and jumping around like a fool.

During his ordinary tasks he was more closely united with God than when he put these aside to do his monastery's assigned retreat exercises, which usually left him with a profound spiritual dryness.

As years passed, he expected—and held as his worst fear—that some severe physical or mental suffering would cause him to lose the conscious awareness of God that he had experienced for so long. However, God's kindness reassured him that they would never leave him, and would give him the strength to bear any harm that Love would allow to happen to him. Knowing this, he feared nothing and had no need to communicate with anyone concerning the state of his soul. If and whenever he did try communicating his soul's state to others, he always came away feeling more perplexed. Because he was willing to give up his life and lose himself for the love of God, he feared nothing. Complete surrender to God is the sure way, and there is always light to guide us.

In the beginning, we must act faithfully and renounce ourselves, but after that, we experience only unspeakable joy. When we face difficulties, we only need to return to Jesus and ask him for his kind help making everything easy.

Often we settle for penances and private devotions, neglecting love, which is our purpose, our meaning, and our end. Our works prove this neglect, and that's why we see so little solid goodness.

We don't need skill or special knowledge to approach God. We only need a heart resolved to devote itself only to them or for them, and to love only God.

ONGOING CONVERSATION

FOURTH CONVERSATION

NOVEMBER 25, 1667

Brother Lawrence talked to me with great enthusiasm and openness about his way of approaching God. Some of it I've already written down.

He told me its essence: Let go once and for all of everything we recognize as not tending toward God. That makes space for us to practice and become accustomed to an ongoing conversation with them, without ceremony or strategy. All we need to do is recognize Love's intimate presence within us, speak with them in every moment, and ask for God's help. To know Love's intent in ambiguous situations, that's all we have to do. Then we can carry out those things we clearly see Love asks of us, by offering our tasks to God before beginning, and when our tasks are completed, by thanking God for finishing.

During this ongoing conversation, we engage in praising, respecting, and constantly loving God for their infinite kindness and excellence.

Without consulting our thoughts, we must confidently ask for God's grace, relying on our Friend's infinite goodness. At every opportunity, God presents us with Love's grace. Brother Lawrence saw this clearly. He only lacked this awareness when he was distracted from God's company, or if he forgot to ask them for their help.

In times of doubt, God always gives light when our sole intention is to please them and act for their love.

The refining process that develops our soul does not depend on changing our works, but on doing for God what we would ordinarily do for ourselves. It's a pity to see how many people get attached to doing certain works very superficially, to gain something or someone's good opinion, always confusing the means for the end.

He found no better way of going to God than by the ordinary tasks that were prescribed to him by obedience, disentangling these as much as he could from all self-interest and concern for others' opinions, and doing all work for the simple love of God.

It's a serious misconception to think of set times of prayer as being different from any other time. We want to be as closely united with God by action during times of work, as we are by prayer during times of prayer.

His set times of prayer are now the practice of God's presence, where his soul shelters and rests from everything but love. He hardly notices any difference outside of these times, since he always holds himself close to God, praising and blessing them with all his strength, spending his life in constant joy, though he still hopes God may give him something to suffer when he is stronger.

We rely on God and give ourselves solely to them, for they will not deceive us.

Don't get tired of doing little things for the love of God. They consider not the importance of the work but the love. We shouldn't be surprised if at first we are frequently distracted. Eventually, we'll develop the habit that helps us act in love without thinking about it, and with great pleasure.

Only cultivate faith, hope, and love. These root us solely in God's intentions. All other things are irrelevant, and we shouldn't settle, but rather view these as a bridge, not stopping there but crossing over quickly so by trusting and loving we can lose ourselves in our sole meaning.

Everything is possible for those who believe, even more for those who hope, still more for those who love, and most of all for those who practice and persevere in these three powerful paths.

Our purpose is to become the wisest lovers of God in this life, as we hope to be for all eternity.

When we take up the spiritual life, we need to think deeply about who we are. We will find ourselves deserving criticism, undeserving of the name *Christian*, and vulnerable to all sorts of problems and endless setbacks. These upset us and make our health, moods, affections, and outward behaviors uneven. These show we are human, people God wants to teach humility through an endless number of internal and external troubles and anxieties.

Once we understand this, why should we be surprised that we experience suffering, temptation, conflict, and arguments from our neighbor? Instead, we must surrender ourselves to these and bear everything as long as God wants us to, just as we would anything we find beneficial.

Our soul is increasingly dependent on grace as we aspire to a higher spiritual maturity.

4

THE HEART OF BROTHER LAWRENCE

THE PRACTICE OF THE PRESENCE OF GOD, A SUMMARY

COMPILED BY JOSEPH OF BEAUFORT,
TAKEN FROM LETTERS AND SPIRITUAL MAXIMS
WRITTEN BY HIS FRIEND BROTHER LAWRENCE

TRANSLATOR'S INTRODUCTION
TO *THE HEART OF BROTHER LAWRENCE*

Translated and made available here for the first time for a general audience, *The Heart of Brother Lawrence* crystallizes in 1,200 words the friar's best advice on practicing the presence. It exists largely because his friend and editor Joseph of Beaufort needed some text to fill out part 2 of the first print edition of 1694. Even adding its twelve pages, that edition of the book reached only ninety pages. Beaufort created it mainly from his friend's *Letters* and *Spiritual Maxims*, titling this short section *The Practice of the Presence of God*. Since it represents the friar's essence, I renamed it *The Heart*, also to avoid the confusion of a section's sharing the book's main title.

To enter this book's history yourself, almost at the very beginning, any reader can find the two parts of the first edition free online by searching "maximes spirituelles bibliotheque nationale de france" for the 1692 edition 1, part 1, and "les moeurs et entretiens laurent google books" for the 1694 edition 1, part 2. You don't need capitalizing, nor the aigu accent (*è*) in *bibliothèque*, nor the linguistic ligature *o et e collés* (*œ*) in *mœurs*. You too can click through sepia pages that are over three centuries old. I owe a debt of gratitude to the Bibliothèque Nationale de France for publishing these digital versions that are gateways to the seventeenth century.

On first seeing the brown-green abstract cover of the 1692 book, with its shapes evoking swirling oak trees, then after clicking to open it, and discovering blue-brown marbled end papers, I felt an awe. While I was quarantined at home during the pandemic, with limited travel, I still imagined the fragrance of tannin and time-seasoned paper, there in a deep library silence. My own sensory engagements were coffee brewing and, with fewer cars on the roads, more bird songs, and an ever-present feeling of collective grief.

I was surprised by how intimate these editions feel. Even via screens. A patient, skilled typesetter added typographic ornaments in both hand-sized duodecimo editions. These are cheerful. Sandwiched between the publisher's Paris address at the bottom of the copyright page, and the book's long title that begins with the all-caps *MAXIMES SPIRITUELLES*, we find two hedera leaves (ivy) called "floral hearts." Each chapter begins with a decorative rectangular heading made of several rows of stars and plant-scrolls, plus ornaments mark chapter ends. It's magical, such craft.

Opening *The Heart of Brother Lawrence*, an angelic flourish decorates its initial letter "L" in the all-caps "LA" ("THE") in "LA pratique la plus sainte et la plus nécessaire en la vie spirituelle, est la présence de Dieu" (page 79): "THE most sacred and most necessary practice in the spiritual life is the presence of God." This "L" is framed by a diamond shape that is itself framed by a larger square, and along every outer side of the diamond rests an androgynous angel face with wings, four in all. (For those who like the long *s* (ſ), I count six in that first line—in *sainte, necessaire, spirituelle, est, presence.*)

A very similar angelic flourish decorates the "T" in "TOUTES" (page 77) in the 1692 edition, for the "EVERYTHING" that begins *Spiritual Maxims*, announcing: "EVERYTHING is possible for those who believe." The thoughtful simplicity of the printer's craft contributed stillness to the seventeenth-century reader's immersion into the wisdom of Brother Lawrence.

When this piece met its first audience it was received with love for its brevity, style, and relevance. I hope contemporary readers feel the same about *The Heart*.

THE HEART OF BROTHER LAWRENCE

COMPILED BY JOSEPH OF BEAUFORT

The most sacred and most necessary practice in the spiritual life is the presence of God. The essence of this presence is enjoying and becoming used to God's divine company of three Persons, speaking humbly and looking to them lovingly for support all the time, at every moment, without rules or limits, especially in times of temptation, pain, loneliness, exhaustion, and even disbelief and stumbling.

We continue to apply ourselves so that all our actions, without exception, become a kind of brief conversation with God, not self-consciously, but coming from the heart's goodness and simplicity.

We always act deliberately and mindfully, not impulsively or rushed (which are signs of an untrained mind). We work gently and lovingly with God, asking them to accept our work. By our persistent attention to God, we will break the cycle of harmfulness, and make all weapons fall.

During our work and other activities, even during our reading, no matter how spiritual, and even during our external devotions and vocal prayers, we must stop as often as we can—for a brief moment—to love God deep in our heart, savoring grace even though briefly and secretly, praising them, asking for help, offering them our heart, and thanking them.

What can please God more than if we leave all created things many times during the day to withdraw and respect Love present within?

We can offer God no greater evidence of our faithfulness than by frequently detaching and turning from all that is created to enjoy their Creator for a single moment. This practice dissolves gradually, and almost unconsciously, the self-preoccupation that's such a part of human nature.

This presence of God is the soul's life and food, and can be acquired by Love's grace. Here are the ways.

> The first is a great simplicity in living, caring for ourselves compassionately so we avoid doing, saying, or thinking whatever might not please Love, and when it does happen, we humbly ask their forgiveness and offer penance.
>
> Another is a great faithfulness to the practice of this presence and to the inner awareness of God in faith, always doing this exercise gently, humbly, and lovingly, without giving in to any hurry.
>
> Then we take special care that the inner awareness somewhat precedes our activities, that it accompanies these from time to time, and that we finish all tasks in the same way. We must not be discouraged when we forget this sacred practice, for we only need to take it up again calmly. When the habit's formed, we find contentment in all we do.
>
> Also to arrive at this state requires our practice of self-control, since a soul who still indulges in worldly things cannot completely enjoy this divine presence. To be with God, we need to let go of everything in creation.

God wants to live in our heart completely. If we do not
empty it of all that's not God, they cannot act there and
do what they please.

The friar often mourns humanity's blindness. He cries out
ceaselessly that we deserve compassion for settling for so little. "I
have," God says, "infinite treasures to give you, but you're satisfied
with an occasional tangible devotion that does not last very long."
In this way, we tie God's hands, and stop the abundance of Love's
graces.

To advance in the practice of the presence of God we also let
go of all our cares, including a lot of private devotions, very good
in themselves but often done for the wrong reasons. These are no
more than means for arriving at an end. When through this exercise of the presence of God we are present with Love who is our
end, then returning to the means of private devotions is unnecessary. Instead, we continue our loving conversation with God,
resting in the holy presence, sometimes by an act of reverence,
other times by offering ourselves, or thanksgiving, and anything
else our minds can conceive.

To be with God we don't always have to be in church. We can
make our hearts an oratory where we withdraw from time to time
to talk with Love there. Everyone is capable of these familiar
conversations with God.

A brief lifting up of the heart is enough, writes Brother
Lawrence. He recommends this exercise to a gentleman in the
military—a brief awareness of God, an inner act of affection,
though running with sword in hand. These prayers, however
short, are very pleasing to God, and far from making a person
lose courage in the most dangerous situations, are strengthening. This way of prayer is very practical and necessary for a
soldier exposed every day to threats to his life and often to his
salvation.

Keep this practice in mind as often as possible.

This exercise of the presence of God is very useful for set times of prayer. Because its practice stops the mind from wandering during the day, keeping it attentively in God's presence, we find that it becomes easier for the mind to remain still during set times of prayer.

We cannot avoid the dangers and hazards that life is full of without God's constant help. But how can we ask for help unless we are with God? How can we be with God unless we think of them often? How can we think of them often unless we form a sacred habit of holding ourselves in their presence, asking them for the graces we need at every moment?

Nothing can comfort us more in life's difficulties and grief than this intimate conversation with God.

If we practice the presence of God faithfully, all the illnesses of our bodies will become easy to bear. Often God may let us suffer to refine our souls and bring us into rest with them. How can someone who is with God, and wants only God, be capable of suffering? That is why we must respect Love in our weaknesses and in our sufferings, offering God our grief from time to time, asking them lovingly, as a child does a parent, for conformity to their sacred kindness, and for the help of their grace. These short prayers are very helpful for anyone who is sick, and are an excellent remedy for pain.

As long as we are with God suffering is a paradise. In this paradise we become accustomed to continuing this familiar conversation with God even when we are suffering. And we work with our mind to keep it from wandering away from Love. When we are sick, we need to look after ourselves responsibly, so that we do not do, say, or think anything—trying to ease the pain—other than what pleases God. When we are attentive to them in this way, suffering will no longer be anything but softness, balm, and consolation.

These truths of the practice of the presence of God are ones the world does not understand—and I am not surprised. The world sees illnesses merely as natural pains and not as graces from God. Those who consider these as signs of Love's mercy and God's hand, useful for our salvation and healing, ordinarily find great consolation in sufferings.

5

PROFILE

THE WAYS
OF BROTHER LAWRENCE

EDITED BY JOSEPH OF BEAUFORT,
TAKEN FROM CONVERSATIONS AND LETTERS
WRITTEN BY HIS FRIEND BROTHER LAWRENCE

TRANSLATOR'S INTRODUCTION
TO THE *PROFILE*

What sets the *Profile* apart from other texts in the book is the beautiful way Joseph of Beaufort shares new insights and additional quotes taken from his conversations with Brother Lawrence. From the priest's faithful notetaking after their tête-à-têtes, special lines emerge. For instance, without the *Profile* material, we wouldn't meet these words from the friar: "I flip my little omelette in the frying pan for the love of God."

Reading the *Profile* we come closer to the humble friar and his wisdom. Through this additional record of his conversations, we also sense the healthy intimacy of his relationships. Beaufort is careful not to reuse materials from the *Last Words* eulogy, his first account of his friend's spiritual journey, repeating here only the eulogy's narration of his friend's last illness and death, because he valued how calmly the friar faced both. I'm glad he did because that valedictory passage merits and rewards rereading.

Originally titled *Les Mœurs du Frère Laurent*, or *The Ways of Brother Lawrence*, where *mœurs* is cognate with Latin *mōrēs* (*mores*), for "ways of behaving, character, morals," the *Profile* later became informally called *The Ways*, or *The Life of Brother Lawrence*, or simply *The Life*, as Archbishop François Fénelon refers to it in his letters. I retitled it the *Profile* because the piece reminds me of *New Yorker* and other "profiles" that give us a sense of a person's selfhood in just a few pages.

New passages include Beaufort's comparison of the friar to a "true Christian philosopher," where earlier translations often omitted these paragraphs. Beaufort cites two classically educated Christian theologians and philosophers, second-century Clement of Alexandria (and his writings from *Stromateis* or *Miscellanies* book 7, chapter 12), and fourth-century Gregory Nazianzus (referencing his *Oration* or *Sermon* 26, paragraph 13). By placing the friar in a context of revered Christian theologians/philosophers, he makes a case for the friar's approach having a revered spiritual ground. Clement, Beaufort notes, defines prayer as an inner silent conversation with a God who never stops listening to the heart's dialogue, and Clement knows prayer as integral to Divinity's relationship with people, which he views as one of friendship, love, intimacy, and union through prayer. For curious readers who want to seek out these works and contexts, this translation includes brief in-text citations for both. The text also corrects Beaufort's two in-text references to Gregory's "*Or.* 28" and "*Or.* 29" to the accurate single reference to *Oration* 26, paragraph 13.

In the *Profile*, Beaufort's description of Brother Lawrence also refers to a religious controversy of that day: "It would be, I believe, helpful to recognize him as an excellent model of genuine compassion now in a time when almost everyone finds worth where there is none, and takes false paths to get there." The phrase "false paths" refers mostly to Quietism, a seventeenth-century Christian philosophy condemned as heresy by the Catholic Church. Fortunately, the friar had friends in high places ready to defend his writings against such charges. Publishing his work required official authorization, seen in the 1694 edition's closing "Permission" page, with its November 17, 1693, statement of approval from Monsignor Louis-Antoine de Noailles, the bishop of

Châlons-sur-Marne (and Beaufort's superior), who pronounced: "We recommend that all persons wanting to acquire true piety read it [the *Profile*], because the example and maxims of this faithful friend of God will benefit everyone greatly."

Quickly becoming treasured text, the *Profile* was often read and shared among the friar's friends. Archbishop Fénelon loaned a countess his copy, assuring her in an August 5, 1700, letter that he was "in no hurry" to get it back. In the *Profile* Fénelon is mentioned by Beaufort anonymously as a "very important man" visiting the friar. Fénelon describes this visit to the countess: "I went to see him [Brother Lawrence] when he was very sick yet very cheerful [*fort malade et fort gai*], and we had an excellent conversation about death. You'll find it briefly here in this book [the *Profile*], though the author doesn't mention me by name."

Due to the preponderance of masculine pronouns, historically the Christian tradition's pattern, and in order to invite women further into the text here, I included a woman philosopher in the "philosopher paragraphs," choosing "she" pronouns for "the wise Christian" they describe, rather than the default *homme* in French with *il* for "he."

What emerges for readers with the *Profile* is a deepening of our sense of the friar as a "lover of wisdom," which we also remember is the etymology of *philosopher* (philo-sophia).

PROFILE

EDITED BY JOSEPH OF BEAUFORT

I am writing down what I myself have heard and seen of the ways of Brother Lawrence, a Discalced Carmelite friar who died about two years ago in the monastery at Paris. His memory is a blessing.

I was asked to write this by someone who rather late in life chose to reside humbly, in last place in God's house rather than keep his higher rank in the world. He preferred the disgrace of Jesus over empty spectacles and worldly luxuries. Since he knew I had collected Brother Lawrence's teachings, he asked me to share these with souls disillusioned by loving the worthless values of the present age.

Even though we have already given the public a *Eulogy* and some *Letters* by this good friar, I'm happy to do that. I believe we cannot share too widely what we have preserved from this holy man.

It would be, I believe, helpful to recognize him as an excellent model of genuine compassion now in a time when almost everyone finds worth where there is none, and takes false paths to get there.

Brother Lawrence will speak for himself. I will give you his own words taken from the conversations I had with him, which as soon as I left him, I wrote down. No one can portray true people of faith better than these individuals, themselves. St. Augustine's *Confessions* and his *Letters* give us a much more authentic portrait than anything that could be said about him. In the same way, hearing what our friar himself said from the simplicity of his heart brings you closest to this friend of God. Nothing I could say could better help you see his spiritual strengths.

The virtue of Brother Lawrence never made him harsh. His goodness made him gentle. He was a warm, welcoming person. He gave others confidence. When you met him, you felt you could tell him anything. You knew you'd found a friend. As for him, once he knew the person he was dealing with, he spoke freely and showed great kindness. He said simple things, but these were always to the point, and full of common sense and meaning. Once you got past his rough exterior, you discovered a unique wisdom, an openness of mind and a spaciousness beyond the reach of an ordinary lay brother. His depth of insight exceeded all expectation. When he was out asking for alms, he showed such good business sense that you could see he had a mind fit to conduct the most serious undertakings. And you could consult him on anything. This was the outward impression Brother Lawrence gave.

He himself has explained his attitudes and his inner life in the conversations I've given you here in this book. As you find described there, his conversion began with a high opinion he conceived of the power and wisdom of God, the loving Trinity, which he carefully cultivated by faithfully shooing away every other thought.

Since this first awareness of God became in time the ground of all Brother Lawrence's perfection, or spiritual maturity, pausing here for a moment is a good idea, to consider how he developed this awareness. The only light he ever used to know God was faith. That was true for him not only at the outset of his spiritual journey, but also from then on, and throughout his entire time at the monastery. In order to learn the ways of God, he wanted to be taught and guided only by faith. He told me several times that everything he heard from others, everything he found in books, and even everything he wrote himself, seemed bland in comparison to what faith revealed to him of the great abundance of God and Jesus.

"Only God," he said, "can make themself known as they really are. We seek in arguments and study—as if staring at a poor copy—what we neglect to see in an excellent original. God paints themself in the foundation of our souls, but we don't want to see them there. We leave Love for foolish things like banter, while we refuse conversation with our Sovereign who is always present in us."

"It's not enough," continued Brother Lawrence, "to love and know *of* God from what books tell us, or from how we feel about God in our souls, or from a few fleeting impressions of devotion, or even from some insight. We must animate our faith, and by faith lift ourselves above our feelings to love God and Jesus in all their divine perfections, as they are in themselves, fully perfect, or wholly Love. This way of faith is the spirit of the church, a loving community, and it's all we need to reach a high degree of perfection, or maturity, in love."

The friar contemplated God not only as present by faith in his soul, but also in all that he saw and in all that happened, he immediately lifted his thoughts, going from the creature to the Creator. A dry, barren tree he saw one winter lifted him up suddenly to God, impressing on him such a sublime awareness of Love that it was just as strong and vivid in his soul as the moment he received it forty years ago. He exercised this awareness at every opportunity, so he only used visible things to reach the invisible.

For the same reason, of the little reading he did, among all other books he preferred the holy gospel, because in the very words of Jesus he found he could nourish his faith more simply and clearly.

That is how Brother Lawrence began his practice of the presence, by frequently cultivating in his heart this exalted awareness of God's presence, contemplated by faith. By continual acts of adoration, love, and requests for our Friend's help in what he had to do, he sustained this conversation. Then after completing a task he thanked God. And he asked forgiveness for his oversights, admitting these, as he said, without bargaining with God.

Since these spiritual acts were in this way connected with his daily tasks, and since his tasks provided material for these acts, he did his work more easily. Rather than diverting him from his work, his prayers helped him do it well.

He admitted, however, that at first he had difficulty with this prayer. As he began, he had long periods of time when he was not mindful of this practice, but after humbly confessing his lapse, he took it up again with no trouble.

Sometimes a crowd of wandering thoughts shoved in and seized the place of his God, but he was happy to dismiss these gently and return to his ordinary conversation. In this way his persistence was rewarded with a continual awareness of God. His different and multiple acts were changed into a unified vision, into an enlightened love, into an uninterrupted joy.

"Times of activity," he said, "are no different from times of prayer. I possess God as calmly in the commotion of my kitchen, where sometimes several people are asking me for different things at the same time, as I do when on my knees before the Blessed Sacrament. My faith sometimes even becomes so bright I am blinded by its dazzle and think I have lost it. When that happens, it seems to me that the curtain of obscurity is drawn aside, and the endless and cloudless day of the next life begins to dawn."

This is what our good brother's faithfulness to this practice accomplished. Because he regularly rejected all other thoughts, he made space and time to stop, open up, attend to, and rest in an ongoing conversation with God. Eventually he made this way of being with God so familiar that he said it became almost impossible for him to turn away from God to take up anything else.

In his conversations you find an important comment on this subject. There he reminded us that the presence of God must be sustained by the heart and by love rather than by the mind and by discourse: "In the way of God, thoughts amount to little when compared with the will's actions. Love accomplishes everything," as he said.

"It's also not necessary," he continued, "to have great things to do."

I am describing for you a lay brother in the kitchen, so let me use his own expressions: "I flip my little omelette in the frying pan for the love of God. When it's done, if I have nothing to do, I prostrate myself on the floor and love my God who gave me the grace to do it. After that, I get up happier than a king. When I can do nothing else, it is enough for me to pick up a straw from the ground for the love of God."

"We look for methods," he continued, "to learn how to love God. We want to get there by I don't know how many different practices. We go to such great lengths, trying to remain in the presence of God by so many methods. Isn't it much shorter and more direct to do everything for the love of God? Can't we use all the ordinary tasks of our life to show our love to God and to keep alive our awareness of their presence in us by this exchange of our heart with theirs? We don't need special skills. We only need to go to God, plain and simple." (I have carefully kept his everyday expressions.)

We must not think, however, that to love God it is enough for us to offer them our daily tasks, ask for their help, and do acts of love. Our brother arrived at such a high level of love only because he was most careful from the beginning to do nothing that might upset God. Renouncing everything but God, he completely forgot about himself.

"Since I entered religious life"—and these are his words—"I no longer think about spiritual strength or my salvation. After giving myself totally to God to atone for my sins, and after renouncing everything that is not God out of love for them, I believed that the only task left for me to do for the rest of my days was to live as if only God and I existed in the world."

This is how Brother Lawrence began the spirit life. He chose the most perfect way, leaving all for God, and doing all for their love. Forgetting himself completely, he no longer thought about heaven or hell, or his past sins, or his present ones, after he had asked God for forgiveness. He did not go back over his confessions. He entered a perfect peace once he had confessed his sins to God, and that was all he could do. After that he gave himself freely to God, as he said, "for life and for death, for time and for eternity."

"We are made for God solely," he said, "and they can only be pleased when we leave our preoccupations to attend to Love."

He continued, "In God we can see what we lack, better than glimpsing it with all our introspection. In fact, analyzing our shortcomings may be what remains of our self-absorption, masquerading as spiritual maturity, which still attaches us to ourselves and stops us from lifting our awareness to God."

Brother Lawrence said he never wavered from his initial determination, not even during the four years of his life when his anxiety was so intense that no one could have changed his conviction that he would be damned. Without thinking about what would become of him, and without worrying about his suffering, as all souls in pain do, he consoled himself by saying: "No matter what happens—come what may—I will at least ensure all my actions are done for the love of God for the rest of my life." By forgetting himself, he was willing to lose himself for God, wherein he found his soul content.

His love of God's intentions had taken the place in him of the attachment we ordinarily have to our own. Whatever happened to him, he only saw God's plan in it, which kept him in a continual peace. When we told him about some terrible injustice, rather than being shocked by it, he was instead surprised that there weren't more injustices, given humans' capacity for malice. He would immediately lift his awareness to God, knowing that God could remedy the situation, still allowing these for inscrutably divine reasons. Confident that Love is very just, and is still active in the world, after he prayed for those involved, he didn't worry about it anymore, and remained in peace.

With no advance warning I told him one day that something of great importance, and very close to his heart, on which he had worked for a long time, could not be carried out, and in fact a decision had been made against it. In very simplicity he responded to me, "We must believe that those who made the decision have good reasons. We must carry it out and not talk about it anymore." That is exactly what he did, and so completely that he never said another word about the matter, even though he had many opportunities.

A very important man went to see Brother Lawrence, when the friar was seriously ill, and asked him which he would choose if God offered it: having more time in this life to increase his merits, or being welcomed into heaven. Without hesitation, the good brother answered that he would leave the choice to God. As far as he could tell, he was supposed to do nothing but wait in peace for God to show their will.

This disposition left him with such great indifference to all things and in such complete freedom, that it resembled the attitude of the blessed. He was of no party. You could find no preference or any inclination in him. Our natural attachments, even for the most sacred places or for one's country, did not preoccupy him. He was equally liked by those who held opposite opinions. He wanted the common good for all, unrelated to which people were doing the good or who was receiving it. A citizen of heaven, nothing halted his spiritual progress on earth. His views were not limited to time. By contemplating the Eternal One for so long, he had become eternal like them.

Everything was equal to him—every place, every task. Wherever he was, whatever he was doing, he was content. The good brother found God everywhere, as near him when repairing sandals, as when praying with the community. He was not eager to go on retreats, because in his ordinary work he found the same God to love and respect as in the remotest desert.

His sole way of going to God was to do everything for their love, so it did not matter to him what he did, this task or another one, as long as he did it for God. It was God, not the thing itself, that he considered. He knew that the more opposed to his natural inclination the work was, the more valuable was the love with which he offered it to God. The smallness of the thing in no way diminished the worth of his offering, because God, needing nothing, considers only the love accompanying our works.

Another characteristic of Brother Lawrence was his extraordinary calm, which in another profession would have been called fearlessness. It revealed a wise soul raised above the fear and hope of all that is not God. He admired nothing, was surprised by nothing, and feared nothing. His stability of soul came from the same source as all his other spiritual strengths. The high opinion he had of God showed Love to him as they really are—as unlimited justice and infinite kindness. Relying on these qualities, he was certain God wouldn't deceive him. They would only do him good, since he'd resolved to do his part, focusing only on pleasing Love, doing and suffering everything for their love.

Who was his spiritual director, I asked him one day. He told me he had none and didn't think he needed one, since the *Rule* and his religious responsibilities showed him what his external duties were, and the wise teachings of Jesus asked him to love God with all his heart. Once he realized this, a spiritual director seemed unnecessary to him—but a confessor was greatly needed to forgive his sins.

Those who conduct themselves in the spiritual life by only following their own preferences and opinions, and who believe nothing is more important than pondering whether or not their devotion is good enough—this sort of temperament has difficulty becoming grounded or having certainty for the path. That's because such things change continually, either by our own negligence or by God's direction, for God varies the gifts and actions we receive according to our needs.

The good friar, on the other hand, was steady on the path of faith, which never changes. He was always the same person. Even-tempered, because he focused all his energy on carrying out the duties of the place where God put him, and he only counted the inherent positives of his monastic state as his reward. Instead of paying attention to his own preferences and pondering the road he was walking, he looked solely at God, his journey's end and meaning. So he made great strides toward Love by practicing justice, kindness, and humility. He focused more on doing than on analyzing what he was doing.

Resting on this solid foundation, his devotion was not subject to visions or other extraordinary phenomena. He was convinced that these, even when genuine, most often suggest a weakness of soul settling for God's gifts rather than seeking God themself. Except for the time of his novitiate, he experienced nothing like this; at least he said nothing about it to those he most trusted and opened his heart to. He walked all his life in the footsteps of God's friends along faith's sure path. He never strayed from the ordinary way leading to salvation by the timeless practices taught by the church, by the exercise of good works and the strengths of his monastic state. He was skeptical of all else.

His good sense, and the light he drew from the simplicity of his faith protected him from all the hazards encountered by so many in the spiritual life. Many souls today are shipwrecked against these, surrendering to a love of novelty, their own fantasies, intrigue, and the world's opinion.

Nothing is easier than avoiding these dangers, when we seek only God. In matters of religion, we carefully consider anything that seems new. A very simple intent to seek God and their kindness is not among those things improved over time; instead, the teachings on love are perfect and have been perfect—whole and healing—from their origin. Jesus taught the loving community of faith everything essential, either directly, or by the Holy Spirit speaking to his students. When we want to find our place of safety, we must return to seeking this love in community.

It's true that—in addition to this faith written down and taught orally—the body of Jesus is present on earth in those faithful to his loving teachings. This community needed a living interpreter to explain Love's intentions and be a guide on the path when doubts arise. The Savior our Healer provided for this. He left us the church, a community of kindness, speaking through the body of Love's shepherds. He gave these leaders the mission of explaining and advocating for Love's wisdom, and advising every genuine seeker in the wise teachings of faith, which is the way that can heal us. The faith of this loving community is the sure way that keeps the soul in complete peace, fulfills all its longings, and fully consoles the soul in its exile.

If we are not happy with the wise teachings of faith and want to expand these, if we want to ignore views and devotions supported by faith in exchange for what the church merely "allows" in yielding to its children's weakness, if anxiety and prying make a person give up everything to follow the example of some individual straying from the ordinary way, or if we want to follow our own priorities, preferring our own assumptions to the living wisdom of the loving church, then we deliberately expose ourselves to danger. We become companions of those who are lost, led astray by choosing an illusion.

God—after speaking through the mothers, fathers, and prophets—then spoke through their own son, who teaches us today through the church. The faith this loving community teaches is authentic, abundant, and wise. Let's hold on to it. This holy friar followed it closely, and he provides us in his person with an excellent model of the way that leads directly to God, without detours.

Prepared by such a life, and following such a sure way, Brother Lawrence had no anxiety when he saw death approach.

He had remarkable patience throughout his life, but it got even stronger as he neared his end. He never seemed to have a moment of grief or distress, even when his illness was the most painful. Joy showed not only on his face, but also in the way he spoke. This made the friars who visited him ask if he truly was in pain.

"Pardon me," he said to the brothers. "I *am* in pain. The spot on my side hurts me, but my spirit is content."

"But," they added, "if God wanted you to suffer these pains for ten years, would you still be content?"

"I would be," he said, "not only for that number of years, but if God wanted me to endure my sufferings until the day of judgment, I'd willingly agree. And I would hope for God to give me the grace to be content always."

As the hour approached for him to leave this world, he often cried out, "O, Faith, Faith!" expressing faith's excellence in a few words. He loved God continually, and he told one of the friars he hardly believed any more in the presence of God in his soul because through this bright faith he already saw and experienced something of God's intimate presence.

His courage was so great during this most frightening transition that he said to one of his friends who asked him about it, that he did not fear death, hell, God's judgment, or any destructive forces.

His brothers so enjoyed hearing him say such edifying things, that their questions continued. Didn't he know, someone asked, that it was a terrible thing to fall into the hands of a living God, because no matter who you are, you cannot know for sure if you are worthy of love or hate.

"I agree," he said, "but I wouldn't want to know, for fear of being vain. Nothing is better than giving ourselves to God."

After Brother Lawrence received the last sacraments, a friar asked him, "What are you doing and thinking now?"

"I'm doing what I will do for all eternity," he said. "I am blessing God, I am praising God, I am worshipping God, and I am loving them with all my heart. Our whole profession, friends, is this. We worship God and love them, without worrying about anything else."

Not long after those last words of his heart, Brother Lawrence died, peacefully and calmly, just as he had lived. His death came on February 12, 1691, when he was almost eighty years old.

Nothing gives us a better example of a true Christian philosopher, or friend of wisdom, than what has just been relayed about the life and death of this good friar. Down through history, such people truly renounced the world and dedicated themselves solely to cultivating their spiritual growth through knowledge of God and Jesus, Love's Son. These spiritual seekers took the Good News as their rule of life and professed the sacred philosophy of the Cross.

That's how St. Clement of Alexandria describes these seekers to us (*Stromateis* 7.12). Perhaps he had someone like Brother Lawrence in mind when he said that the main work of the philosopher, which is to say, of the wise Christian, is prayer.

Clement goes on to say that this wise person prays everywhere, not using many words, but secretly in the depths of her soul, while walking, talking, resting, reading, or working. She praises God continually, not only in the morning when she gets up, and again at noon, but in all her actions she is thanking God, like the seraphim of Isaiah. This attention to spiritual things through prayer makes her gentle, friendly, patient, and at the same time, wise in resisting temptation, not allowing pleasure or pain to control her. The joy of contemplation feeds her constantly, without making her full, and keeps her from wanting earth's empty pleasures.

She lives, through love, with God, even though her body still appears on earth. Having experienced by faith this hidden light, she no longer has a taste for things of the world. She is already where she wants to be, desiring nothing, because she has the object of her desire, as much as possible here.

She has no need to put on a tough exterior, because nothing in this life bothers her. And nothing can turn her away from God's love. She does not need to calm herself, because she never gives in to disappointment, convinced that all is well. She doesn't get angry, or upset, because she always loves God and only turns to Love. She's never jealous, because she lacks nothing. In friendship, she goes beyond the human to love the Creator in all creatures. Her soul is solid, and constant, and free from change, because forgetting everything else, she gives her attention totally to God.

To this philosopher's portrait I would like to add a brush stroke from the hand of a wise teacher who was more enlightened by the light of an excellent faith that he shared with Brother Lawrence than by all knowledge gained from the academy in Athens. You may think it odd that I bring together here teachers and scholars with an obscure lay brother, but in the simplicity of the friar's words we find what the brightest lights of the religious community have taught us about the simplicity of Love's ways. All of these sages gained this teaching from Jesus, who hides from the all-knowing and the smug, revealing his wisdom to the little children.

There is nothing more powerful and more indomitable than true philosophy, as St. Gregory Nazianzus says (*Oration* 26.13).

Everything yields to a philosopher's generosity of spirit. Even if you deprive a philosopher of all the world's comforts, she has wings that lift her up, and she raises up, and takes flight to God, her only teacher.

You can't defeat God, nor an angel, nor a philosopher. Although composed of matter, a philosopher does not seem material, because her soul is vast. Although she has a body, she lives on earth like a celestial being. She is calm in the middle of total chaos. A philosopher allows herself to seem defeated in everything, except in the greatness of her courage. In seeming to give way to those who wish to erase her, a philosopher surpasses and gains a place above her opposers. She no longer clings to the world or its attachments. She makes use of life's comforts only as much as is needed. She limits her dealings to God and herself.

Her soul lifts her above all visible things, and like a clear mirror, reflects the divine image simply, with nothing mixed in of the world's coarseness. Every day she adds the light of new insights to the wisdom she's already gained. Until one day she finally reaches the source of light that we draw from only in the next life, when the brilliance of the truth breaks through the obscurity of all mysteries, dispelling darkness. It is then she reaches the highest happiness.

Here we recognize the qualities of our lay brother, and all those like him.

Although Brother Lawrence lived a hidden life, everyone, whatever their personal circumstances, may benefit greatly from his example given here. He teaches all of us engaged in the world to turn to God, to ask for the grace to carry out our duties and to handle our concerns. He shows others how to turn to God in all conversations and even during times of recreation. By the friar's example, we will be moved to thank God for our blessings and the good that Love helps us do, and we will humble ourselves before God for our stumblings.

This is not a theoretical devotion only to be practiced in the cloister. This prayer is practical. Everyone must adore and love God. We cannot carry out these two important and necessary duties without having a heartfelt conversation with God, where we are turning to Love in every moment, like children who have difficulty supporting themselves without their mother's constant, present help.

This prayer is not difficult. It's easy and necessary for everyone. And this practice is what St. Paul teaches to the faithful, when he says, Pray without ceasing. If we do not practice it, we cannot be aware of our own needs or weaknesses. We cannot know who we are or who God is, or know our constant need for Jesus of Nazareth.

Business and other matters of the world don't excuse us from this duty. God is everywhere. We can talk with God anywhere. Our hearts can speak with Love in a thousand different ways. With a little love, we won't find this difficult.

Those living in monastic communities, removed from life's struggles, have even more to gain from the way that Brother Lawrence lived. Largely freed from the concerns and obligations still burdening those engaged in the world, nothing can stop us from imitating this good brother. We can let go of any thought except for one: doing all things for the love of God, and we can give God all for all, as the friar says.

When we look to the example of his general detachment, his complete forgetfulness of self (so much so that he quit thinking about his salvation to devote himself totally to God), his indifference to the kinds of jobs and duties assigned to him, and his freedom in the spiritual exercises—together these can benefit us all.

6

LAST WORDS

EULOGY HONORING
BROTHER LAWRENCE, 1614–1691

BY HIS FRIEND JOSEPH OF BEAUFORT

TRANSLATOR'S INTRODUCTION
TO *LAST WORDS*

The first sheets lifted by the puller from the printing press in 1692, their ink still wet, included those for *Last Words*, the eulogy written by Joseph of Beaufort, by that time vicar general. He had lost his friend Brother Lawrence a year earlier, on Monday, February 12. In this memorial speech, we see his sincere love for the friar. Beaufort was about fifty-six when his friend died at the age of seventy-seven, and he delivered this eulogy either on or after the friar's burial on Tuesday, February 13, the day before *La Saint-Valentin*, or Valentine's Day, which seems appropriate for the friar of *amour*.

Clearly written by a dear friend, *Last Words* provides an intimate biographical sketch of Brother Lawrence. We learn of his love for nature. He was "often filled with wonder" seeing "the Creator's power, wisdom, and kindness" there, and he wrote "many lyrical and tender things about the grandeur of God" and "only loaned these out reluctantly."

Readers learn here of the friar's calmness when facing death. Beaufort describes his friend's last illnesses from the viewpoint of someone often there with him. We also learn that the friar told several people that he would die before the end of February 1691, as we also saw in his late letters. He had that sense. He knew.

We can tell that the intelligent Beaufort was a very busy vicar general because he transposes in memory two poignant words in his friend's last letters. This slight bobble is valuable, because it reveals something about the friar's attitude toward death. In discussing his friend's letters of "January 22" and "February 6" (Letters 15 and 16), written to the friar's neighbor, the Daughters of the Blessed Sacrament nun, Beaufort says that his friend closed these by saying "goodbye" or "*adieu*"; however, there is no "goodbye" in Letter 16 on February 6. This other "goodbye" is in Letter 14 of December 21, 1690, where the friar wrote, "Goodbye. I will help you with my prayers, poor as these are." This "goodbye" seems to have moved in Beaufort's memory to Letter 16, where it does perhaps make more logical sense. We might expect that a person would say goodbye in what they think is their very last letter, but that was not the friar's style.

To me, as I translated, it makes sense that the friar did not say goodbye in Letter 16, his final handwritten conversation, penned six days before his death. His parting words to this nun, his friend, show that he did not see dying as an ending, and he was empathetic with her to the last. She was his contemporary, and he knew that she had her own mortality on her mind. He considered also her long-term pain and suffering. His focus as he signs off was on comforting her, and reminding her to practice the presence: "I cannot thank God enough for the little bit of relief you have received. I hope in Love's mercy for the grace of seeing God in a few days. Let us pray for each other."

This kind of empathy helps us understand why such a heartfelt eulogy like *Last Words* was written by a very busy vicar general who felt lucky to count himself the friar's friend, lucky enough to spend so many hours of his last weeks together.

LAST WORDS

BY HIS FRIEND JOSEPH OF BEAUFORT

Wise books remind us that Love's welcome is unending, never shortened. God's mercy cannot be exhausted by our needs. The power of God's grace is no less strong today than at the birth of faith. Since God, the loving Three-in-One mystery, wanted the uninterrupted company of a kind community of seekers, they were not content only with the births of extraordinary people in the earliest centuries. Still from time to time they awaken those who completely fulfill the double duties of giving worship worthy of Love's wonder and majesty, and of being models of gentleness. These souls preserve the freshest wisdom of the Spirit, and then transmit it to others, reviving love.

In this eulogy I am celebrating Brother Lawrence of the Resurrection, a Discalced Carmelite friar. God brought him into the world in our times to show the respect Love deserves and to wake up our community in the practice of spiritual wisdom by the rare example of his faith.

Before he entered the monastery, his name in the world was Nicolas Herman. His father and mother were good people who led exemplary lives. Both inspired in him a respect for God from childhood on, taking special care with his upbringing by teaching him solely the sacred principles as reflected in the gospel.

He was born in Hériménil in Lorraine. The military conflicts of this territory entangled him in adversity. He joined the army, living simply and with integrity, and God preserved him with kindness and mercy. He was taken prisoner by German troops on the march, and he was accused of being a spy. Even in this extremely hostile situation, his patience and tranquility persisted. Who can imagine how far these were tested? The soldiers then threatened to hang him. He answered fearlessly, however. He asserted that he was not a spy as the soldiers suspected. He told his captors that his conscience was clear, because he was not guilty of any crime, so he viewed death with indifference. Hearing that and seeing his courage, the officers released him.

The Swedes also made an incursion into Lorraine. While passing through the area, Swedish troops attacked the small town of Rambervillers. There our young soldier was wounded, and his injury forced him to retreat to his parents' home nearby.

Because of this experience, he left the military profession to take up a more sacred way of life and to follow the teaching of Jesus of Nazareth. His decision to turn away from this tumultuous occupation was not motivated by an empty enthusiasm of an immature devotion. Instead, genuine feelings of compassion led him to resolve to give himself completely to God, and to change and to atone for his past conduct. The God of all compassion who destined Herman for a holier life let him glimpse the nothingness of the world's vanities. And then touched him with the love of celestial things.

These first impressions of grace, however, did not immediately achieve their full effect. He often relived in his mind the dangers of his days in military service, the emptiness and corruption of the times, the instability of other people, the treason of an enemy, and the betrayal of his friends. He experienced intense reflection, hard inner struggles, tears, and sighs. Only after that was he finally convinced by the power of eternal truths. He firmly resolved to practice the wise teachings of Jesus consistently. He would follow in the footsteps of his uncle, a holy Discalced Carmelite lay brother who helped his nephew see that the air of the world is contagious. If it does not kill those who breathe it, at the very least it impairs or contaminates the integrity of anyone who follows its ways.

The wise counsel of this enlightened spiritual director opened the way of Love's perfection to Herman, who also had fine qualities of soul that contributed much to his progress. In his face you could see showing his good sense and wisdom, and these qualities soon lifted every obstacle that life and its distractions often throw at those who want to change their lives. His naturally calm determination motivated him so well that he was lifted up in an instant, as if miraculously. By meditating on the promises of his baptism, the disorders of his youth, the mysteries of his faith in Christ, and especially the Passion of Jesus, which always moved him deeply in contemplation, he was changed into a new person. The humility of the cross seemed more beautiful to him than all the glory of the world.

Stirred by this divine love, he searched for God in the simplicity and sincerity of his heart, as Paul the apostle recommends. His only thoughts were for solitude. He wanted to weep for his faults. Mature enough not to worry that he would be acting impulsively, he considered more than once withdrawing from the world. That became a real possibility for him, as I will explain.

Our friar knew a gentleman of nobility, prosperity, and every other worldly advantage who was still dissatisfied with his privileged life. He was always anxious, even though surrounded by wealth. This gentleman became convinced that only God could satisfy his longings. Choosing gospel poverty over every worldly treasure, he entered a hermitage to taste how sweet God is for anyone truly seeking Love. Our Herman took advantage of this welcoming opportunity and followed him there. His soul, finally weary of leading an unhappy life, began to desire rest. With such a faithful guide, nothing stopped him from withdrawing to the desert. There Christ's love inspired him and dispelled his fears, and he became closer to God than ever before.

However, while the life of a hermit is excellent for consideration by the advanced and the mature, or those more perfected in love, it is rarely best for beginners. Soon our new solitary realized this. He watched joy, sadness, peace, worry, passion, distraction, confidence, and despair, one after another, dominate his own soul, making him doubt the authenticity of his path. At that point, he decided to enter a community and embrace a way of life with a rule that is set—not on the shifting sands of short-lived feelings, but on the solid rock of Christ. This foundation of all religious life would in time reassure and strengthen him against the instabilities of his conduct.

Frightened, however, by the possibility of an endless spiritual struggle, and perhaps tempted by self-doubt, he could not commit himself. Day after day passed, and he became more and more uncertain. Finally, he listened to God once again, who called him with such tenderness. Coming to Paris, Herman asked for the religious habit and was received among the lay brothers of the Order of the Discalced Carmelites. He was given the name Brother Lawrence of the Resurrection.

From the beginning of his novitiate, Brother Lawrence applied himself with much conscientiousness to the practices of religious life. He had a special love for the Blessed Virgin Mary and was especially devoted to her. He had a son's trust in her protection. She was his refuge in all the problems of his life. In the troubles and anxieties that shook his soul, he turned to her, and so he often called her his "good Mother."

He especially dedicated himself to the practice of prayer. No matter how demanding his assigned duties were, he never used these as an excuse for neglecting time for this sacred exercise. The practice of the presence of God, and the love it creates, were his most cherished virtues, and before long he became a model for his fellow novices. The resilient grace of Jesus helped him eagerly embrace penance and seek out the self-discipline that our human nature flees with such dislike.

Although monastery superiors assigned Brother Lawrence the most menial tasks, he never complained, not even once. Instead, grace sustained him in the most disagreeable, tedious jobs, and he was never discouraged by meeting the bitter and harsh. Whatever natural dislike he felt, he accepted willingly. He believed himself fortunate to suffer or be humiliated by following the example of the Savior.

His courage and strong work ethic earned everyone's respect. Seeing how others esteem him and sensing his excellence, the novice master felt it best for the youth's well-being to test the authenticity of his vocation and the resilience of his spirit by increasing his difficulties. He assigned the novice different jobs to strengthen his soul. Rather than being upset by this challenge, Brother Lawrence met and endured it with all the reliability you would expect.

This was proven again on another occasion. A friar came to tell him there was talk of dismissing him from the monastery. This was met with his response: "I'm in the hands of God, and they can do with me as they please. I don't live for the opinions of others. If I can't serve God here, I'll serve them somewhere else."

When the time came for his profession of monastic vows, he did not hesitate. He offered all of himself completely to God. I could record here several generous acts deserving special attention that would convince readers of the fullness of his sacrifice, but I will pass over these in silence to emphasize the inner struggles distressing his soul. These came partly by order of divine Providence, who permitted these to refine him, and partly from his lack of experience, because he wanted to walk in the spiritual life in his own way.

He saw the harms, the sins of his past life, and this sight caused him horror. These memories made him feel so small and so flawed in his own eyes that he judged himself unworthy of the slightest tenderness from the Spouse. He also saw himself, however, as extraordinarily favored, and in the humble awareness he had of his own spiritual poverty, he did not dare accept the heavenly blessings God was giving him. He did not know yet that God is so merciful that they communicate themself to anyone who has sinned and stumbled, as Brother Lawrence knew was true for him.

Then a fear of self-deception began overwhelming his heart, and his spiritual and mental state seemed so uncertain that he no longer knew what would become of him. His doubt caused him such terrible torments, he could only find release by likening these intense anxieties to his understanding of the pains of hell. In this distressing state, he often withdrew to a private place near his pantry where there was an image of Jesus bound to the column. There the friar—his heart distraught, his face wet with tears—poured out his feelings to God, begging Love not to let him perish, since he was placing all his trust in them and had no intention but to please them.

No matter how he prayed to God, however, fear, anxiety, and confusion increased his anguish until suddenly his mind shut down. It was paralyzed. The solitude he had envisioned as a safe haven now seemed a stormy sea. Panicked, his mind tossed like a ship pounded by winds and rain, abandoned by its pilot. He did not know which way to go or how to resolve this. Pulled in different directions, he felt a secret inclination to surrender to God by a continual sacrifice of himself, but his fear of straying from the ordinary path of spiritual maturity made him unintentionally resist Love. All these very human, distressing thoughts filled him with terror. Everything scared him. His soul was plunged in such bitterness and in such thick darkness that he was unable to accept any help, from heaven or earth.

This painful experience stretched him to his limits. Yet God often uses the same to refine the character of their true helpers before sharing the priceless treasures of Love's wisdom. That is what Love did with Brother Lawrence. His patience, gentleness, self-control, determination, and calm during these trials were extraordinary. With his humble self-awareness and behavior, with no inflated idea of himself, he truly valued only suffering and humiliations. He asked only for Love's chalice, and he drank all its bitterness.

If only God had let Brother Lawrence keep some of the reassurance he felt at the beginning of his penance, but no, everything was taken from him. Ten years of fears and churning thoughts gave him no rest. He had no taste for prayer, no softening of his pain. This made his life so heavy to him, reducing him to such an extreme neediness, that he became a burden to himself. His life felt unbearable. His sole support was faith.

This teeming crowd of clashing thoughts reduced our lay brother to extremes, but his courage never left him. Instead, when his sufferings were the most severe, he always had recourse to these: to set times of prayer, to the practice of the presence of God, to the practice of Love's and of the community's intentions, to physical austerities, to sighs and tears, and to long vigils. Sometimes he spent nearly all night before the Blessed Sacrament. Finally, one day Brother Lawrence made an unconditional resolution to bear these, not only for the rest of his life, but for all eternity, if that's what God thought best. He was reflecting on the sufferings that distressed his soul, and realized that his motivation for enduring these was his love of God and fear of displeasing them. Making his resolution, he said, "It doesn't matter to me anymore what I do or what I suffer so long as I remain lovingly united to God's intentions, which is my only concern."

That was exactly the attitude God wanted him to have so they could fill him with Love's graces. From that moment on, the resolution of the friar's heart increased more than ever before. Then God, needing neither time nor much thinking to make themself understood, suddenly opened the eyes of Brother Lawrence. He saw a ray of divine light illumining his mind, dispelling all his fears, and ending his suffering. Then the graces he received more than compensated for all his struggles in the past.

"The world seems very small to a soul who contemplates the greatness of God," St. Gregory the Great wrote. And that is how the friar experienced it. A few words from the letters Brother Lawrence wrote to a Carmelite nun attest to this:

> The entire world seems incapable of keeping me company. All that I see with my physical eyes just passes before me like phantoms and dreams, while everything I see with the eyes of my soul is my only desire. Finding myself still too far away from it causes my distress and anguish. Dazzled on the one hand by the brightness of this divine Sun of justice who scatters the shadows of the night, and on the other, blinded by the muck of my miseries, I am often beside myself. However, my most usual occupation is to remain in the presence of God with all the humility of a weak but loyal helper.

This holy exercise of the practice of the presence shaped Brother Lawrence's special character, and the habit he formed with it became so natural to him that he spent the last forty years of his life in an actual exercise of the presence of God, or, as he himself described it, in a silent and intimate conversation with them. He explains the practice in some of his letters and other writings.

One day a religious superior asked him how he had acquired the habit of the presence of God, as the practice seemed so easy and so constant for him. Obliged to reply, our lay brother answered him:

When I entered religious life, I saw God as the intent and end of all the thoughts and loves of my soul. At the beginning of my novitiate, during the hours assigned to interior prayer, I spent my time learning to appreciate the truth of this divine Being by the wise light of faith, rather than by the work of meditation and many words. By this short and sure way, I advanced in the knowledge of this kind Presence with whom I resolved to remain forever. So, completely filled by the wonder of this infinite Being, I would enclose myself in the place that obedience had marked out for me, the kitchen. There, alone after taking care of the pantry and other necessary preparations for my duties, I gave what time remained to prayer, both before and after my work.

When I began my tasks, I said to God with a child-like trust: "My God, since you are with me, and since you ask me to apply my mind to these external duties, I beg you, give me the grace to remain with you and keep you company. But so my results will be better, my Friend, work with me, accept my actions, and occupy all my affections."

Then during the task, I continued to speak intimately with God, offering them my little services, and asking for their graces. When finished with my work, I examined the way I'd done it, and if I found any good in it, I thanked God. If I noticed any shortcomings, I asked forgiveness for these, and without getting discouraged, I redirected my mind and began anew to remain with God as if I'd never moved away. That's how, by getting back up after my falls, and by many little acts of faith and love, I came to a state where it would be just as impossible for me not to think about God as it was difficult in the beginning to get used to doing so.

Just as Brother Lawrence experienced the great benefits that this holy exercise brings to the soul, so he advised all his friends to practice it with as much attention and dedication as possible. To encourage his friends to embrace it with a firm resolve and unstoppable courage, he presented such strong and convincing reasons, that not only did he persuade their minds, he touched even as far as their hearts. He convinced his friends to love and embrace this sacred practice with as much enthusiasm as previously it had been seen with indifference.

In addition to the gift of his words to persuade those who came to him, he also had his good example. You only had to look at him to become a better person and to put yourself in the presence of God—even if you were in a hurry.

He called the practice of the presence of God the shortest and the easiest way to reach Love's perfection, the form and essence of goodness, and the great defense against wandering into harm or into harming.

He assured us this exercise—and forming a habit of its practice—only required courage and a good intention. He proved this truth even better with his actions than with his words: We all noticed how he lived. When he served as a cook, even in the middle of his very demanding work, including the most distracting tasks, his mind and spirit were recollected in God. Although his duties were challenging and difficult, often requiring him to do by himself what two would usually do, you never saw him hurry. Instead, with remarkable composure, he gave each thing the time it needed. Always keeping his humble, calm manner, he worked without being slow and without being rushed. He stayed in the same evenness of spirit and constant peace.

He carried out these assigned kitchen duties with the greatest love possible for about thirty years, when Providence directed otherwise. His superiors assigned him to an easier task—as sandal maker and repairer—as a large ulcer developed on his leg. This change gave him more leisure to adore God in spirit and in truth as he preferred, letting him cultivate—or perfect—a more mature awareness of God's presence by this exercise of faith and love.

In this intimate union developed solely by faith and love, the images of creatures and created things, so hard to unsee, faded from his imagination. The powers of hell, which never stop opposing us, no longer dared attack Lawrence, as they did during his decade-long dark night of the soul. His passions became so tranquil that he became hardly aware of these anymore. If sometimes these provoked some little emotion to humble him, then he resembled those high mountains that only see storms forming at their feet.

From that time on, some ten years after entering the monastery, he seemed naturally inclined to goodness, maintaining a sweet temperament and complete integrity—all with the best heart in the world. His kind face, his understanding and warm ways, and his simple, modest manner immediately gained him the respect and goodwill of all who observed him. When you yourself practiced the presence of God more, then you learned that the more you saw him, and the more closely you looked at his life, the more you discovered in him a depth of honesty and devotion rarely found elsewhere.

People noticed that he did not try to call attention to himself in any way. He always followed the simplicity of community life, without putting on a melancholy and austere air only serving to discourage others. He was not one of those inflexible people who consider holiness incompatible with good manners. He was down-to-earth. He associated with everyone and was kind to his brothers and friends, never acting like he was special.

Far from boasting of God's graces and trying to make his goodness visible to attract others' admiration, he consistently applied himself to leading a hidden, unknown life. Just as the arrogant seek every possible way to obtain an advantageous place in the minds of others, we can see that a truly humble person makes every effort, not only to avoid the applause and praise of others, but even to discredit the honorable estimations some might have of him. We have seen God's friends in the past do deliberately ridiculous things to attract scorn and mockery from everyone, or at least to inspire doubts as to the high opinions some form of another's worth. That is what Brother Lawrence did. His humility, which I consider his special trait, made him sometimes find sacred strategies and some apparently childish behaviors to disguise his goodness and hide its brightness. He did not seek glory, but reality. As he wanted only God to witness his actions, he wanted only God as his reward.

Although Brother Lawrence was very reserved about talking about himself, he was willing to speak with his brothers for their edification, not with the most enlightened ones, whose knowledge and incredible insights often inflate their hearts, but with the little ones and the simplest. We noticed that when he found people of this caliber, he hid nothing from them. With remarkable simplicity he taught the most beautiful secrets of the inner life and the treasures of divine wisdom. The spirit accompanying his words so strongly moved those benefiting by conversation with him that his friends came away fully satiated by the love of God, and completely motivated by the immediate desire to put into practice the great truths taught in private by Brother Lawrence.

Since God led him more by love than by fear of any judgments, his spiritual conversations inspired this same love of disengaging from the slightest attachments to creatures, and of letting one's old self die in order to establish the power of the new self.

He said to his brothers,

> If you want to make great progress in the spiritual life, don't pay attention to the attractive words or subtle discourses of the experts on earth. Regret follows those who only want to satisfy their curiosity with human knowledge. The Creator teaches the truth, instructs the hearts of the humble in a moment, and enlightens the humble persons to understand more things about the mysteries of faith and also of the Divinity, than if for many years you had analyzed such mysteries.

For this reason he carefully avoided replying to questions of idle curiosity that go nowhere, only working to clutter the mind and dry up the heart. When, however, his superiors demanded he openly state his thoughts on the difficult questions raised during these spiritual conversations, he answered so well and with such clarity that no one could refute his replies. That is what several experts, priests and friars, noticed while requiring him to answer their questions. This was also the informed opinion of an illustrious bishop of France, whose conversations with Brother Lawrence convinced him to speak in favor of the friar. This bishop said that Brother Lawrence had made himself worthy for God to talk with him interiorly and reveal their mysteries to him. He added that the abundance and sincerity of the friar's love for God made him live while on earth like the blessed do in heaven.

The friar rose to God by an intimate knowledge of creatures and of all Creation. He believed that the books in the most famous schools only teach a few things in comparison with the great book of the world, if we know how to study it well. His soul, touched by the diversity of the world's various elements, was drawn to God so strongly that nothing could separate him from Love. In each of the earth's marvels he noticed the different traits of the Creator's power, wisdom, and kindness. These delighted his spirit, often filling him with wonder. When feelings of love and joy lifted up his heart, these made him cry out with the Prophet: "My Sovereign, God of gods, how incomprehensible you are in your thoughts, profound in your designs, and powerful in all your actions!"

Brother Lawrence wrote many lyrical and tender things about the grandeur of God and the ineffable ways they communicate their love to our souls. He only loaned these out reluctantly and on condition his writings be returned as soon as possible. His friends who saw some of the sheets taken from what he wrote down were so delighted and enlightened, that these were always discussed with much admiration. Although he tried to hide his work, still we were able to collect a few fragments. I regret we couldn't find everything he wrote.

Judging as best we can by what little remains of his letters and spiritual maxims, we have every reason to believe, as he said himself to one of his friends, that these little works are in the truest sense outpourings of the Holy Spirit and products of God's love. Sometimes after he expressed these feelings on paper, when he compared what he had just written with what he experienced within, he judged his writings so inferior and so far removed from his high awareness of God's mystery and kindness that he often felt it necessary to rip up everything right then and there. He was more than willing to shred these, because he only wrote to release his pent-up feelings. He wanted to let his spirit soar, and open wide his and chest, too narrow for the divine fire that devoured him, causing a strange kind of suffering. As water in a too-small basin overflows, or as a strong fire trapped underground finds a way out and then releases, so was his experience with the Holy Spirit.

Among the many spiritual strengths flourishing in Brother Lawrence, faith was among the most important. Those who value justice live by it, and his faith was the life and nourishment of his spirit. It helped his soul grow so much that he made significant and visible progress in the spiritual life. This beautiful strength put all the world under his feet and made it so lowly in his eyes that he did not think it worth taking even the lowest place in his heart. Faith led him to God, and raising him above all created things, sent him searching for happiness solely in God's friendship. Truth was his best teacher. And faith single-handedly taught him more than if he'd read every book in existence.

Faith gave him this high regard for God and this deep reverence for the sacred mysteries, especially for the most Blessed Sacrament of holy communion at the altar where the Child of God lives and rules. So devoted was Brother Lawrence that he spent many hours there, day and night, on his knees, offering God love and reverence. This same faith gave him profound respect for the Word of God, for the community of seekers and sacred teachings, and for his superiors, whom he obeyed as representing Jesus.

In fact, he believed with such certainty the truths showed by faith that he often said, "All the beautiful speeches I hear about God, everything I read about Love, and all that I feel for them—none of this can satisfy me, for God is infinite in their perfections and thus is ineffable. No words have enough energy to give me a perfect idea of God's greatness. Faith reveals God to me and lets me experience them as they are. I learn more in this way in a very short time, than I would in several years of schooling."

"O Faith! O Faith!" he also would cry out. "O awesome strength! You illuminate our human mind, and lead to friendship with our Creator! Kind strength, how little known you are, and even less practiced, though knowledge of you is so splendid and so helpful."

From this living faith came his certain hope in God's kindness, his childlike trust in God's providence, and his total and all-embracing self-surrender into God's hands. He did not even worry what would become of him after his death, something we will see in more detail when we consider his attitude and the feelings he experienced during his last illness. During the greater part of his life, he was not content with basing his salvation passively on the power of God's grace and the worth of Jesus of Nazareth. Instead, he forgot himself and all his own interests, and in the Prophet's words, he threw himself headlong into the arms of infinite mercy. The more hopeless things seemed to him, the more he hoped. He was like a rock that when beaten by the waves of the sea becomes a stronger refuge in the middle of the storm.

We already saw this when we spoke of the inner struggles God sent to test his loyalty soon after he entered religious life. If, in St. Augustine's words, the measure of hope is the measure of grace, what can we imagine about the grace God shared with Brother Lawrence, which empowered him, as Scripture says, to hope against hope? That is why he said that the best reverence you can give God is to completely question your own strength and to trust perfectly, or totally in God's protection, because this is how to make a sincere confession of our own weakness and a true acknowledgment of the Creator's omnipotence.

Love is the queen and soul of all spiritual strengths. Love gives these their excellence and value. That is why we are not surprised by the perfection that is the mature goodness possessed by Brother Lawrence, because God's love ruled so perfectly in his heart. As St. Bernard says, he had turned toward this divine object in all his affections. If faith helped him see God as the highest truth, and if hope helped him contemplate God as his ultimate end and complete happiness, love showed him that God is the most perfect of all beings, or more precisely, that God is in fact perfection, or Love.

Far from loving God for some personal benefit, his love was so disinterested that he loved God even when there was no suffering to avoid or reward to gain. Wanting only the sincerity of

God and their approval, he made the accomplishment of God's sacred meaning his paradise. This is something we see even in his final illness. His spirit was so free, even until his last breath, that he explained the feelings of his heart even then as if he were in excellent health.

The purity of his love was so great that he wished, if it could've been possible, that God would not see the actions he was doing to serve Love, so he could do these only for Love's intention and without any return to himself. He complained lovingly, telling his friends that God would let none of his actions go by without immediately rewarding him a hundredfold, often giving him such great experiences and tastes of their divinity that he was sometimes overwhelmed by these gifts. This made him say with his usual respect and familiarity: "It's too much, God! It's too much for me. Please give such favors and consolations to anybody who's wandered off, and to any who don't know you, to draw these to your service. I have the happiness of knowing you by faith. That should be enough for me, I think. But, because I shouldn't refuse anything from a hand as rich and generous as yours, I accept, my God, the favors you do for me. After receiving these, I return to you what you gave me. Please be kind enough to accept these from me. As you are well aware, I don't seek or want your gifts, but I seek you yourself. I can't settle for anything else."

This simplicity of love and detachment only served to stir his heart more and intensify the divine fire's flames. Their sparks sometimes reflected out from him. Even though he made every effort to hide the powerful movings of divine love burning within him, sometimes he was powerless to stop their projections. Despite his best intentions, we often saw his face visibly aglow.

When he was by himself, however, he let the fullness of this fire move, crying out: "God, give more room and openness to the abilities of my soul, so I can have more space to express your love. Or else support me and sustain me with your omnipotent goodness, because otherwise I will be consumed by the flames of your love."

When he was talking with his brothers, he often turned to God, lamenting the time he lost in his youth: "Kindness, so ancient and so new, I loved you too late! Don't do the same, my brothers. You are young. Learn from my sincere confession. I cared too little about serving Love during my early years. Devote all yours to Love. I think back on how, if only I'd known God earlier, and if only I'd been told the things about God I'm telling you now, I wouldn't have delayed so long in loving them. Believe me, and count for lost all time not spent in loving God."

Since the love of God and the love of neighbor are one and the same practice, through the love he had for God, we can estimate his love for his neighbor. He was convinced by what Jesus said in the gospel, that the smallest kindness done for the least of God's friends was done for God themself. So he took special care to serve his friar brothers in all his assigned duties, especially while working in the kitchen. There he provided what was needed for the friars' physical well-being according to the poverty of their monastic state. His happiness came from pleasing his friends as if they were angels. He inspired this same love in all who succeeded him in this job.

He helped the poor in their need, doing everything in his power that he could. He listened to and comforted those who were suffering, and he helped with his counsel. Even as they worked to earn a living, he encouraged heaven as their intention. In short, he did all the good that he could for his neighbor, and he never hurt anyone. He became everything to everyone to bring all to God.

As St. Paul says, love is patient: love triumphs over all difficulties, and love suffers everything for the love of the beloved. Can we doubt the patience Brother Lawrence had in his weaknesses, in his illnesses, and in his difficulties with disability, when he loved God so perfectly, so completely? In fact, according to the same apostle, patience has a beautiful rapport with love. For just as love is the path of perfection, or spiritual maturity, so patience is that which sustains us on that path. Patience holds, considers, keeps, delivers, and completes Love's work—*opus perfectum habet*. Patience, or the Presence, is the simple, ongoing, persevering practice of returning to God. Do we need anything more to convince us of the perfect, whole, and holy state to which God raised Brother Lawrence?

We see proof in how he practiced these two spiritual necessities of love and patience during the extremely painful illnesses God let him experience. We won't go into detail here about how he suffered from a kind of sciatic gout that made him limp and tormented him for nearly twenty-five years, and how this later degenerated into a leg ulcer that caused him intense pain. Here I want to focus mainly on three major illnesses that God sent him during the last years of his life to prepare him for death and make him worthy of the reward intended for him.

The first two illnesses were devastating. These severely weakened him, but he endured both with remarkable patience. He kept the same evenness of spirit in the middle of these sufferings as when he was in the most vigorous health. In the first case, he expressed some desire for death. Speaking with the physician after his fever went down, he told him: "Ah, Doctor, your remedies work too well for me. You only postpone my happiness!" In his second illness, he seemed not to have any preference. He remained completely indifferent toward life and death, perfectly resigned to God's decisions. As happy to live as to die, he wanted only what pleased God's divine Providence to decide.

During the third illness, however, I can tell you that he showed signs of an altogether extraordinary constancy, acceptance, and joy. This illness separated his soul from his body, reuniting it with his Beloved in heaven. As he had been longing for this blessed moment for so long, when he saw it come, he felt much satisfaction. The sight of death that frightens and throws the toughest person into absolute terror, did not intimidate him at all. He looked at it with a confident eye. We can even say he defied it. For when he saw the humble bed prepared for him, and when one of his friends confirmed that yes it was for him, saying: "It's for you, Brother Lawrence. It's time to leave," he replied, "It is true. There is my deathbed. But someone who hardly expects it will follow me soon."

That is exactly what happened, just as he said it would. Although this friend was in perfect health, he became sick the next day and died on the same day Brother Lawrence was buried. The following Wednesday then, this friar was buried in the same grave. The love that had united these two good brothers during life did not seem to want to separate the friends in death, because no other place for burial could be found but the common grave.

Four or five months earlier Brother Lawrence had told several people he would die before the end of February. He wrote two letters, two weeks apart, to a nun of the Daughters of the Blessed Sacrament, whose convent garden bordered monastery property. The first one dated January 22, he finished with these words: "Goodbye. I hope to see God soon." In the second, dated February 6, the day before he fell ill, he finished his letter with these words: "Goodbye. I hope in Love's mercy for the grace of seeing God in a few days."

On the same day that he took to his bed, he told a friar, one of his close friends, that his illness would not last long, and that he would leave this world very soon. He was so sure of the day of his death that the next day, which was a Friday, he spoke more precisely, and told one of the friars he would die the following Monday. And it happened as he said.

Before we turn to the circumstances of his death, and the last thoughts and feelings he expressed on his deathbed, let's return to the constancy he showed in his illness. Having only one desire left, to suffer something for the love of God, he repeated what he'd said many times during his life, that his only suffering was that he'd not had any. He found comfort knowing there was a purgatory, because at least there he would suffer something to atone for his sins. So when he found a favorable opportunity for atoning in this life, he did not let it escape. He turned on his right side deliberately, knowing it would be very painful, and he wished to stay there to satisfy his intense desire to suffer.

The brother looking after him wanted to give him some relief, but the friar told him twice: "Thank you, Brother, but please let me suffer a little for the love of God." In this painful state, he said passionately: "My God, I love you in my infirmities. This is how I'll suffer something for you, my God. In your good time, let me suffer and die with you."

Then he often repeated these verses of Psalm 50: "*Cor mundum crea in me, Deus; ne projicias me a facie tua; redde mihi laetitiam salutaris tui*," etc.: "Create in me a clean heart, God. Do not turn your face away from me, but give me back the joy of your salvation."

Pleurisy caused the unusual pain he felt in this position, on his right side; he would undoubtedly have died if the nurse had not arrived just in time. This brother saw the problem at once and turned him on his other side, enabling him to breathe more freely. So passionate was he about suffering that it became his greatest comfort. He never seemed to have a moment of distress even during the worst suffering of his illness. His joy showed not only on his face, but even in the way he spoke, which made the friars visiting him ask if he truly was in pain.

"Pardon me," he said to the brothers. "I *am* in pain. This spot on my side hurts me, but my spirit is content."

"But, Brother," one replied, "if God wanted you to suffer these pains for ten years, would you still be content?"

"I would be," he said, "not only for that number of years, but if God wanted me to endure my sufferings until the day of judgment, I'd willingly agree. And I would hope for God to give me the grace to be content always."

Such was Brother Lawrence's patience at the beginning of, and during the progression of his final illness, which lasted for four days.

Then as the hour came for him to leave this world, his spirit strengthened. His faith became more alive, his hope more solid, and his love more incandescent. You could discern the intensity of his faith by his frequent exclamations showing his special appreciation for its loyalty: "O, Faith! O, Faith!" he said, expressing faith's excellence in a few words. Filled with faith's power and illumined by this light, he loved God continually and described how this love took place naturally in him. He once told a friar he hardly believed any more in the presence of God in his soul because through this bright faith he already saw and experienced something of God's intimate presence.

The firmness of his hope was no less obvious. His courage was so great during this most frightening transition that he said to one of his friends who asked him about it, that he did not fear death, hell, God's judgment, or any destructive forces. In fact even as he saw a shadow coming and going around his bed, Brother Lawrence laughed at it.

His brothers so enjoyed hearing him say such edifying things, that their questions continued. Didn't he know, someone asked, that it was a terrible thing to fall into the hands of a living God, because no matter who you are you cannot know for sure if you are worthy of love or hate.

"I agree," he said, "but I wouldn't want to know, for fear of being vain." He focused so much on surrendering that, forgetting himself and considering only God and doing Love's will, he would say, "Yes, if by some miracle, you could love God in hell, and they wanted to put me there, I wouldn't care, because God would be with me, and their presence would turn it into a paradise. I have given myself to Love. God can do with me as they please."

If he loved God this much during his life, he loved them no less at his death. He made ongoing acts of love, and when a friar asked him if he loved God with all his heart, he answered, "Ah, if I knew my heart did not love God, I would tear it out right now."

His pain increased visibly. The brothers brought him the last sacraments. He received these joyfully, fully conscious. This lucidity stayed with him until his last breath. Although his loving brothers rarely left him alone for a moment, day or night, giving him all the help he could expect, his friends did also let him have some privacy so he could rest a little and collect himself during the last precious moments of life, to reflect on God's great grace given in the last sacraments. He used these moments wisely to ask God for the final perseverance of their sacred love.

A friar asked him, "What are you doing and thinking now?"

"I'm doing what I will do for all eternity," he said. "I am blessing God, I am praising God, I am worshipping God, and I am loving them with all my heart. Our whole profession, friends, is this. We worship God and love them, without worrying about anything else."

A friar commended himself to Brother Lawrence's prayers and pressed him to ask God to give the friar the true spirit of prayer. Brother Lawrence told the brother that he must give God his cooperation, and work on what he could himself to become worthy of it. These were the last words of his heart.

The next day, Monday, February 12, 1691, at nine o'clock in the morning, fully conscious, without agony or convulsions, Brother Lawrence of the Resurrection died in the kiss of Love and returned his soul to God with the peace and tranquility of someone asleep.

His death was like a gentle sleep helping him pass from this hard life to a blessed one. So if we can guess what follows death from the sacred actions that preceded it, what other impression can we have of Brother Lawrence, who left this world loaded down with kind deeds and merits? It is easy to believe, and presume without flattery, that his death was so dear to God that its reward was ready and waiting. He lives among Love's friends. Presently he enjoys God's company. His faith has been recompensed by clear vision, his hope by going home, and his earthly kindness by consummated love.

LAGNIAPPE

TIMELINE
NICOLAS HERMAN | BROTHER LAWRENCE

APPENDIX A

Year	Age	Event
1614		Nicolas Herman's birth in the duchy of Lorraine, village of Hériménil, 345km east of Paris, 4km south of Lunéville, with his birth year on record, but no birth month or date.
1618–1648	4–34	The Thirty Years' War. A series of religious wars that began between Roman Catholics and Protestants raged in central Europe, with the loss of eight million lives, civilians and soldiers, from combat, disease, and starvation—and exacerbated by plague and climate change.
1628	14	"Without a summer." First of two seventeenth-century years with temperatures so low that many crops never ripened.
1628–1631	14–17	First bubonic plague in seventeenth-century France. Loss of some two million souls over three epidemics.

Year	Age	Event
1632	18	Herman's cosmic vision. Seeing a barren tree in winter, he received "a profound awareness of God's kindness and power that never left his soul."
c. 1633	c. 19	Herman's soldiering. Enters Thirty Years' War.
1634–1661	c. 19–47	France occupation of Lorraine. Perhaps influences Herman to join the local Lorraine military.
1635–1640	21–26	Herman's leg injury. Wounded at the siege of Rambervillers. Leaves military service because of war injury. Works in Paris as a footman for Monsieur of Fieubet. Fails as a hermit. Struggles with anxiety and spiritual confusion.
1636–7	22–23	Second bubonic plague in seventeenth-century France.
1640	26	Herman's entrance into Paris monastery. Enters in mid-June as a lay brother.
1640	26	Herman's receiving brown Carmelite habit in mid-August. Takes religious name, Brother Lawrence of the Resurrection.
1640–1642	26–28	Herman's two-year novitiate starts mid-August. Helps in monastery kitchen.
1640–1650	26–36	Ten-year dark night of the soul for Brother Lawrence.

Year	Age	Event
1640–1690	26–76	Little Ice Age—the longest, most severe period of global cooling in the Holocene era, causing death of up to one-third of the entire human population.
1642	28	Profession of vows by Brother Lawrence on August 14. Likely becomes cook in training.
1643–1715	29–death	Louis XIV's seventy-two-year reign—known as the Sun King.
1645–1660	31–46	Principal cook. Brother Lawrence assigned to make meals for more than one hundred friars.
1647–1650	32–36	Worst years of anxiety.
1648–1653	34–39	French civil wars posed threats to the Ancien Régime, foreshadowing the 1789 revolution.
1650	36–death	Inner peace for over forty years achieved by Brother Lawrence by practicing the presence prayer.
1660	46–death	Large leg ulcer. Likely developing from war injury, this ulcer changes Brother Lawrence's life. His superiors reassign him as monastery sandal maker, moving him from the kitchen as principal cook to the *savaterie*, or sandal shop, where he repairs some two hundred sandals of Discalced Carmelites. During this time, he occasionally helps in kitchen, not as principal cook but with menial tasks such as peeling vegetables to help for special occasions or feast days.

Year	Age	Event
1665	51	Wine merchant trip. Makes three-week, eight-hundred-kilometer round trip to Auvergne to buy wine for friars.
1666	52	Wine merchant trip. Travels by river on a six-hundred-kilometer trip to Burgundy, again to buy wine for the monastery.
1666	52	First visit by Priest Joseph of Beaufort (c.1635–1711). On August 3, the friar and Beaufort have the first of several conversations, included in this book.
1666–1691	52–death	Increasingly painful leg disability. The friar's intense leg pain increases during his last twenty-five years, likely from war injury.
1668–9	54–55	Third bubonic plague in seventeenth-century France.
1670	56	France invasion of Lorraine again.
1670s–1680s	56–76	Quietist controversy in France, Italy, and Spain.
1672	58	Extreme spring season drought.
1675	61	"Without a summer." Second of two seventeenth-century years with temperatures so low that many crops never ripened.
1689–1691	74–77	Loss of mobility. Brother Lawrence is unable to walk during the last twenty-four and a half months of his life.
1690	76	Vicar-general appointment for Joseph of Beaufort. At the end of the friar's life, his friend Joseph of Beaufort is appointed vicar general of the bishop of Châlons-sur-Marne.

Year	Age	Event
1691	77	Brother Lawrence's death. On February 12, in Paris, the friar dies at the Discalced Carmelite Monastery, Rue Vaugirard.
1692		First edition, part 1, published. The French first edition, part 1, includes *Note to the Reader, Eulogy (Last Words), Spiritual Maxims,* and *Letters.*
1693–4		Historic weather takes many lives. Winter ice and summer rains cause suffering "'unknown in the memory of man'" and "'without parallel in past centuries.'"
1694		First edition, part 2, published. The French first edition, part 2, includes *Ways (Profile), Conversations,* and *The Practice of the Presence of God (The Heart of Brother Lawrence),* a summary of the friar's teaching, taken from his *Spiritual Maxims* and *Letters.*
1699		Second edition published. Works of Brother Lawrence are sandwiched in with Quietists' writings. This anthology shares themes of walking with God, practicing the presence, and the baby-at-the-breasts image for this prayer. The second edition opens with a Genesis 17:1 quote in Latin at the frontispiece: "*Ambula coram me, & esto perfectus,*" and underneath it in French: "*Marchez en ma presence & soyez parfait,*" traditionally, "Walk in my presence & be perfect," and that

Year	Age	Event
1699 (cont.)		I translate, "Walk with me, and be wholehearted, mature, and kind." Adding context to the friar's use of the breast/*mamelle* image in Letter 2, this volume has an example by the Quietist Jeanne-Marie Guyon (1648–1717), who uses that same image for praying the presence. I translate it: "Stay as silent as possible. A small child attached to the breast shows this to us while nursing. First a child moves their little lips to bring in the milk, but when the milk starts to flow in abundance, this child is content to swallow it without doing anything new because that would spread the milk and stop the nourishment" (33).
1700		Brother Lawrence's work spreads. Knowledge of his teaching is also spreading via letters after his death in 1691. In the August 5, 1700, letter to the countess of Montbéron, Archbishop of Cambrai François Fénelon also includes the breast image learned from Brother Lawrence, among others, comparing the nourishment of practicing the presence to a baby's nursing at the breast (*mamelle*). The archbishop noted his respect for the friar as an advanced spiritual teacher, and supported his teaching during and after his lifetime. It was Fénelon who contributed considerably to the posthumous international spread of the humble friar's teaching.

EYEWITNESSES: ON THE CATASTROPHIC SEVENTEENTH CENTURY

APPENDIX B

"A third of the world has died."

> —Abbess Angélique Arnauld, letter,
> Port-Royale-des-Champs,
> France, 1654

"There have been so many deaths that the like of it has never been heard in human history."

> —Hans Conrad Lang, *Tagebuch* [*Diary*],
> South Germany, 1634

"[P]lague contaminates the air."

> —Jean-Nicolas de Parival, *Short history
> of this Iron Century*, Brussels, 1653

"Those who live in times to come will not believe that we who are alive now have suffered such toil, pain and misery."

> —Fra Francesco Voersio of Cherasco,
> *Diario del contagio* [*Plague Diary*],
> Italy, 1631

"It was so harsh a winter that no-one could remember another like it."

—Hans Heberle, *Zeytregister* [*Diary*],
Ulm, Germany, 1627

"[N]ever in . . . memory . . . has the like famine and mortality happened."

—East India Company officials, letter,
Surat, India, 1631

"There was great hunger throughout the Christian world."

—Inscription, Old Sambor Cathedral,
Ukraine, 1648

"Because of the [scarcity] sent to us by God, we wanted to sell our property to our relatives, but even our relatives refused, and left us to die from hunger."

—Gavril Niţă, Moldavian peasant, 1660

"Jiangnan has never experienced this kind of disaster."

—Lu Shiyi, *Zhixue lu* [*Diary*],
South China, 1641

"The pryces of victuall and cornes of all sortes wer heigher than ever heirtofore aneyone living could remember. . . . The lyke had never beine seine in this kingdome." ("The prices of food and grain of all kinds were higher than any living person could remember. . . . Nothing like it had ever been seen in this kingdom.")

—Sir James Balfour,
"Some shorte memorialls and
passages of this yeire," Scotland, 1649

"This seems to be one of the epochs in which every nation is turned upside down, leading some great minds to suspect that we are approaching the end of the world."

—Nicandro, pamphlet, Madrid,
Spain, 1643

Adapted from *Global Crisis: War, Climate Change & Catastrophe in the Seventeenth Century*, by Geoffrey Parker.

HORARIUM | THE HOURS
A DAY IN THE LIFE OF BROTHER LAWRENCE, LAY BROTHER

APPENDIX C

Activity	Time
Rise	5:30 AM
Morning Prayer | Lauds	6:30 AM
Mindful Prayer	6:45 AM–7:45 AM
Community Mass	8:00 AM
Breakfast	8:45 AM
Work/Study	9:00 AM–12:00 PM
Midday Prayer	In Private
Community Lunch	12:00 PM
Work/Study	12:30–4:45 PM
Evening Prayer | Vespers	4:45 PM
Mindful Prayer	5:00 PM–6:00 PM
Office of Readings	6:00 PM
Dinner	6:15–7:00 PM
Recreation/Study	7:00 PM

Activity	Time
Night Prayer | Compline	In Private
Sleep	9:00 PM or Earlier

TRANSLATOR'S NOTE

"Mindful prayer" for "mental prayer" is for those who find, as I do, that this monastic phrase sounds negative because of possible slang associations with *mental*. Teresa of Ávila teaches "mental prayer" (*oración mental*) as an intimate, healing friendship with God, grounded in an interior conversation with a loving Trinity. Twice daily, these periods are for silent, meditative prayer. For centuries the word *mental* in the Catholic term "mental prayer" clearly denoted "performed by the mind," as in this Middle English translation of Italian mystic Catherine of Siena: "God schewiþ . . . how a soule schal come fro vocal preyer to mental preyer" ("God shows how a soul can move from vocal prayer to mental prayer") (*Oxford English Dictionary*). But words change. Also, Brother Lawrence doesn't use the phrase "mental prayer," referring instead to Carmelite set times of ("mental") prayer simply as: "my hours of prayer" ("*mes heures d'oraison*"), "my prayers" ("*mes oraisons*"), and "the times of prayer" ("*le temps de l'oraison*"). In the book's text, I translate these twice-daily periods of mental prayer as "set times of prayer." The first of these references, in Letter 2, reads for clarity: "set times of mental prayer," and a reminder in the Second Conversation reads, "set times for the mental prayer of his Carmelite tradition."

This Horarium is adapted from *Discalced Carmelite Vocations* (ocdfriarsvocation.org/).

FRENCH EDITIONS
USED IN THIS TRANSLATION

Laurent de la Résurrection. *Maximes spirituelles fort utiles aux âmes pieuses, pour acquérir la présence de Dieu. Recueillies de quelques Manuscrits du Frère Laurent de la Résurrection, Religieux Convers des Carmes Déchaussés. Avec l'abrégé de la Vie de l'Auteur et quelques Lettres qu'il a écrites à des personnes de piété.* Paris: Edmé Couterot, Rue Saint-Jacques, au Bon Pasteur, 1692.

First edition, part 1: *Note to the Reader* (ā ij–ā vj), *Eulogy* (1–76; here, *Last Words*), *Spiritual Maxims* (77–107), *Letters* (108–181). This beautifully decorated edition, about 4.5 by seven inches, is here: Bibliothèque Nationale de France | Gallica.

Laurent de la Résurrection. *Les Mœurs et Entretiens du Frère Laurent de la Résurrection, Religieux Carme Déchaussé. Avec la Pratique de l'Exercices de la présence de Dieu, tirée de ses Lettres.* Châlons: Chez Jacques Seneuze, 1694.

First edition, part 2: *The Ways* (here, *Profile*; called *The Life of Brother Lawrence*, or *The Life* by François Fénelon, 1–43), *Conversations* (45–77), *The Practice of the Presence of God* (here, *The Heart of Brother Lawrence*) (79–90). It is digitized by permission of Bibliothèque Nationale de France as a Google book.

Laurent de la Résurrection. *Recueil de divers Traitéz de Théologie Mystique qui entrent dans la Célèbre Dispute du Quiétisme qui s'agite présentement en France. Contenant: I. Le Moyen court & très-facile de faire Oraison. II. L'Explication du Cantique des Cantiques. Tous deux par Madame Guion. III. L'Éloge, les Maximes Spirituelles & quelques Lettres du Fr. Laurent de la Résurrection. IV. Les Mœurs & Entretiens du même Fr. Laurent, & sa pratique de l'Exercice de la présence de Dieu. Avec une Préface où l'on voit beaucoup de particularitéz de la Vie de Madame Guion.* Cologne: Chez Jean de la Pierre, 1699; Amsterdam: Henri Wetstein, 1699.

Second edition: *Note to the Reader* (339–341), *Eulogy* (343–382; here, *Last Words*), *Spiritual Maxims* (383–399), *Letters* (399–438), *The Ways* (441–466; here, *Profile*, sometimes called *The Life*), *Conversations* (467–485), *The Practice of the Presence of God* (486–492; here, *The Heart of Brother Lawrence*). The friar's work is included among Quietist writings. Edition dedication: "Genesis 17:1: *Ambula coram me, & esto perfectus. Marchez en ma presence & soyez parfait.*" It is accessible at Bibliothèque Nationale de France | Gallica.

De Sainte-Marie, Father François, OCD, Carmelite priest, ed. *L'Expérience de la Présence de Dieu, by Laurent de la Résurrection* (French edition). Text established by S. M. Bouchereaux; Paris, Éditions du Seuil, 1948.

Sureau, Denis. *Vivre la Présence de Dieu, by Laurent de la Résurrection.* Les classiques de la spiritualité (French edition). Paris: Éditions Artège, 2020.

FURTHER READING AND LISTENING
BROTHER LAWRENCE

De Meester, Conrad. *Frère Laurent de la Résurrection: Ecrits et entretiens sur la Pratique de la présence de Dieu.* Paris: Éditions du Cerf, 1991.

De Meester, Conrad, ed. *The Practice of the Presence of God. Brother Lawrence of the Resurrection: Critical Edition.* Salvatore Sciurba, translator. Washington, DC: Institute of Carmelite Studies, 1994.

De Meester, Conrad. *Vie et pensées du frère Laurent de la Résurrection.* Paris: Éditions du Cerf, 2010.

Fénelon, François. *Oeuvres de Fénelon: Archevêque de Cambrai.* Vol. 2. Paris: Louis Vivés, 1854.

Huxley, Aldous. *The Perennial Philosophy.* New York: HarperPerennial, 1945.

McGinn, Bernard. *The Persistence of Mysticism in Catholic Europe: France, Italy, and Germany 1500–1675.* Volume 6, Part 3 of *The Presence of God: A History of Western Christian Mysticism.* New York: Herder & Herder, 2020.

CONTEMPLATIVE PRAYER

Acevedo Butcher, Carmen. *The Cloud of Unknowing.* 2009. Boulder, CO: Shambhala Pocket Library, 2018.

Acevedo Butcher, Carmen. https://www.carmenbutcher.com/.

Averay, Philip, host. "The Treasures of *The Cloud of Unknowing* with Carmen Acevedo Butcher Pt. 1 and Pt. 2." *Wisdom's Table*, season 1, episodes 11 and 12, 30 March 2021 and 12 April 2021. Podcasts.

Crampton, Georgia Ronan, ed. *The Shewings of Julian of Norwich, Part 1.* Middle English Texts Series: University of Rochester. Kalamazoo, MI: Medieval Institute Publications, 1994.

Frykholm, Amy, host. "Translation as Embodied Mysticism: An Interview with Carmen Acevedo Butcher." *In Search Of,* season 1, episode 1, 1 March 2022. A *Christian Century* podcast.

Holmes, Barbara A. *Joy Unspeakable: Contemplative Practices of the Black Church,* 2nd ed. 2004. Minneapolis: Fortress Press, 2017.

Thurman, Howard. "The Sound of the Genuine." Baccalaureate Address at Spelman College. May 4, 1980. Edited by Jo Moore Stewart. *The Spelman Messenger* 96(4), summer 1980.

DISCALCED CARMELITE SPIRITUALITY

Discalced Carmelite Vocations. Washington, DC. https://www.ocd-friarsvocation.org/.

Egan, Keith J., ed. *Carmelite Prayer: A Tradition for the 21st Century.* Mahwah, NJ: Paulist Press, 2003.

Hunt, Anne. *Trinity: Nexus of the Mysteries of Christian Faith.* Maryknoll, NY: Orbis, 2005.

Hunt, Anne. *What Are They Saying about the Trinity?* Mahwah, NJ: Paulist Press, 1998.

San Juan de la Cruz. *El Cántico Espiritual.* Libro de Dominio Público, 2011.

Santa Teresa de Jesús. *Camino de Perfección.* Public Domain.

Santa Teresa de Jesús. *Las Moradas O Castillo Interior.* FV Éditions, 2020.

Santa Teresa de Jesús. *Libro de las Fundaciones.* Ivory Falls Books, 2017.

SEVENTEENTH-CENTURY FRANCE

Bossenga, Gail. "Estates, Orders and Corps." In *The Oxford Handbook of the Ancien Régime*, edited by William Doyle, 141–166. Oxford: Oxford University Press, 2012.

Chute, Hillary L. *Disaster Drawn*. Cambridge, MA: Belknap Press of Harvard, 2016.

Daudin, Pascal. "The Thirty Years' War: The First Modern War?" *ICRC*. 23 May 2017.

Doyle, William. *The Oxford Handbook of the Ancien Régime*. Oxford: Oxford University Press, 2012.

Moxon, Joseph. *Mechanick Exercises: Or, the Doctrine of Handy-Works Applied to the Art of Printing*. Vol. 2. London: On the West-side of Fleet-ditch, at the Sign of Atlas, 1683.

Parker, Geoffrey. *Global Crisis: War, Climate Change & Catastrophe in the Seventeenth Century*. London: Yale University Press, 2014.

Pasko, Wesley Washington. *American Dictionary of Printing and Book-making, containing a history of these arts in Europe and America, with definitions of technical terms and biographical sketches*. New York: H. Lockwood, 1894.

Russo, Ronald A. *Plant Galls of the Western United States*. Princeton: Princeton University Press, 2021.

Ventura, Gal. "The History of Breast-Feeding in France." In *Maternal Breast-Feeding and Its Substitutes in Nineteenth-Century French Art*. Translator Merav Fima. Leiden, the Netherlands: Koninklijke Brill NV, 2018.

TRANSLATION

ARTFL Project. *Dictionnaires d'Autrefois*. Centre National de la Recherche Scientifique and University of Chicago, 2021.

Briggs, Kate. *This Little Art*. London: Fitzcarraldo Editions, 2018.

Budziszewski, J. *Commentary on Thomas Aquinas's Virtue Ethics.* Cambridge: Cambridge University Press, 2017.

Clement of Alexandria. "Seeking the Face of God: Prayer and Knowledge in Clement of Alexandria," by Henny Fiskå Hägg. In *The Seventh Book of the Stromateis*, edited by Matyáš Havrda, Vít Hušek, and Jana Plátová, 131–142. Boston: Brill, 2012.

Clément d'Alexandrie. *Les Stromates. VII.* Introduction, texte critique, traduction et notes par Alain Le Boulluec. Paris: Les Éditions du Cerf, 1997.

Cotgrave, Randle. *A Dictionarie of the French and English Tongues.* London: Adam Islip, 1611; New York: Georg Olms Verlag, 1970. Assembled from two scans in the French National Library by Greg Lindahl, 2015.

Davis, Lydia. "Translator Profile: Lydia Davis." Interview with Allegra Rosenbaum. *Asymptote.* 24 August 2016.

Gregory of Nazianzus. *Select Orations.* 2003. Translated by Martha Pollard Vinson. Washington, DC: Catholic University of America Press, 2010.

Liachowitz, Claire H. *Disability as a Social Construct.* Philadelphia: University of Pennsylvania Press, 1988.

Mechthild von Magdeburg. *Das fließende Licht der Gottheit.* Stuttgart-Bad Cannstatt: frommann-holzboog, 1995.

Ray, Donna E. *"There Is a Threeness about You": Trinitarian Images of God, Self, and Community among Medieval Women Visionaries*, PhD dissertation. University of New Mexico, 2011.

Valéry, Paul. *Traduction en Vers des Bucoliques de Virgile, précédée de Variations sur les Bucoliques.* Paris: Gallimard, 1956.

Valéry, Paul. "Variations on the *Eclogues*." In *The Art of Poetry*, 295–312. Translated by Denise Folliot. 1958. Princeton: Princeton University Press, 2014.

NOTES

FRONTISPIECE

Brother Lawrence was uneducated and rough. . . . Fénelon, pp. 429–430 (Letter 253).

This translation and all others in this book are by the author.

I'm only asking you to look at Love. . . . Santa Teresa in *Camino*, 26.1–3.

There is in you something that waits. . . . Thurman, pp. 14–15.

INTRODUCTION

FEATHERS AND THE FRIAR'S GROUNDED WISDOM

By laying eggs on oak leaf buds. . . Russo, pp. 20, 9–10, 15, 58, 905.

After these were set in forms. . . . Pasko, p. 35.

Then strong hands took up. . . . Moxon, pp. 306–319.

THE METHODLESS METHOD

Discalced (or "Shoeless") Carmelites. . . . De Meester (1994), p. xxxv.

THE FRIAR OF POTS AND PANS

The friar's attitude resembles. . . . Santa Teresa in *Libro*, 5.8.

NICOLAS HERMAN AND KING LOUIS XIV
The Ancien Régime in France was a threefold, man-made. . . . Bossenga, pp. 141–166.
The clergy was generally. . . . Doyle, p. 4.

NO COUNTRY, NO EDUCATION
We only know his parents' names because. . . . De Meester (1994), p. xlii.

WAR, PLAGUE, LITTLE ICE AGE
It became infamous as. . . . Daudin, n.p.; Parker, pp. 31, 169.
Ten years into this Thirty Years' War. . . . Parker, p. 630.
Quarantine restrictions were mandated. . . . Parker, p. 631.
In his lifetime Herman also experienced five decades. . . . Parker, p. xv.
Climatologists call this period. . . . Parker, p. 3.
It had the coldest weather on record. . . . Parker, pp. 24, 77, 696.

FIVE FEET AND THREE INCHES
Of thousands enlisting in Louis XIV's army. . . . Parker, pp. 22–23.
This "stunting" from starvation also damaged. . . . Parker, p. 323.

INJURIES IN WAR
Les Grandes Misères et les Malheurs. . . . Chute, pp. 39, 48; Parker, p. 31 (plate 2).

WHO BROKE EVERYTHING
Anonymized in *Last Words*, he was Herman's. . . . De Meester (1994), p. 27.

A BARREN TREE IN WINTER AND A DARK NIGHT OF THE SOUL
Further intensifying this experience. . . . Parker, pp. 3, 502.

BECOMING BROTHER LAWRENCE: FROM KITCHEN TO SANDAL SHOP

As a lay brother, he also had a minimal voice in. . . . De Meester (1994), p. xxiii.

If we count his time as cook in training. . . . De Meester (1994), p. 29.

DECADES OF DISABILITY

In the middle of pain Brother Lawrence discovered. . . . Holmes, p. 26.

Holmes knows this joy unspeakable "is not silent". . . . Holmes, pp. xvii–xviii.

Reading *Joy Unspeakable*, her study of. . . . Holmes, pp. xvii–xviii, 29.

THE UNLIKELY FRIENDSHIP AT THE HEART OF THIS BOOK

A young Parisian priest when he first showed up. . . . De Meester (1994), p. 93.

Although Beaufort's father was a rich merchant. . . . De Meester (1994), p. xxxiii.

TRANSLATOR'S NOTE

This intimate process is described vividly. . . . Briggs, location 2288.

And my translating experiences resonate. . . . Briggs, location 2394; Valéry (Denise Folliot), p. 302.

This "labor of approximation," as he called translation. . . . Valéry (Denise Folliot), p. 302.

Philosopher Aldous Huxley said. . . . Huxley, pp. 286–287.

As Teresa of Ávila tells her convent sisters. . . . Santa Teresa in *Las Moradas*, pp. 193–194; also 16, 18, 25, 26, 60 (*misericordia*); 2, 8, 10, 25, 37, 45, 53, 88, 101 (*bondad*); 194 (*divina compañía*); 183, 195 (*hondo/a*); and San Juan in *El Cántico*: 346–347.

This kind divine community of the Trinity.... Hunt (1998), pp. 3, 83.

Mystics like the friar, and thirteenth-century poet Mechthild.... Mechthild, p. 53, 2.19.

In this experience, God is. . . . Hunt (2005), p. 16, and Hunt (1998), p. 44.

Trinitarian spirituality is "intensely relational".... Hunt (2005), pp. 186–187, and Hunt (1998), pp. 81, 44.

SPIRITUAL MAXIMS

TRANSLATOR'S INTRODUCTION

In the friar's emphasis on *amour*.... Crampton, pp. 18, 38, 295.

We also find John.... San Juan in *El Cántico*, pp. 82–83, 172–173 (songs 7 and 17).

LETTERS

TRANSLATOR'S INTRODUCTION

The few letters without dates. . . . De Meester (1994), p. 80 (in footnote 1).

LETTER 1 NOTE

Brother Lawrence addresses this first letter. . . . De Meester (1994), pp. 132 (map), xli (in footnote 27), 130–131.

His *rappeler* for "calling back" holds.... Acevedo Butcher, p. 201.

LETTER 2 NOTE

The friar then moves intentionally.... Santa Teresa in *Camino*, 31.7.

Wet nurses were in such demand.... Ventura, pp. 3-78.

Fénelon recommends . . . "stay at the breast." . . . Fénelon, p. 429 (Letter 253).

A year later he writes, "Return to the breast".... Fénelon, p. 454 (Letter 280).

In another, he presents this prayer as nourishment. . . . Fénelon, p. 429 (Letter 252).

Fénelon also describes practicing the presence as. . . . Fénelon, p. 355 (Letter 182).

LETTER 3 NOTE

In this third letter written to a nun. . . . De Meester (1994), p. 74.

A handful of the friar's surviving letters. . . . De Meester (1994), pp. 61, 74.

LETTER 8 NOTE

Even with the friar's challenges. . . . De Meester (1994), p. 68 (in footnote 3).

LETTER 9 NOTE

In the words he writes. . . . Santa Teresa in *Camino*, Chapter 29.5.

Like Teresa, he also emphasizes. . . . Santa Teresa in *Camino*, Chapter 26.2.

LETTER 11 NOTE

The friar's writing echoes Teresa of Ávila. . . . Santa Teresa in *Camino*, 28.7.

LETTERS 13–16 NOTES

In this next set of letters. . . . De Meester (1994), pp. 132 (map), xli (in footnote 27), 130–131.

This convent was founded in Lorraine in Rambervillers. . . . De Meester (1994), p. 131.

CONVERSATIONS

TRANSLATOR'S INTRODUCTION

On August 3, 1666, a thirtysomething. . . . De Meester (1994), p. 93.

At the time—from 1690 on—he was vicar general. . . . De Meester (1994), p. 88.

Brother Lawrence says in the Fourth Conversation. . . . Santa Teresa in *Las Moradas*, p. 219.

PROFILE

TRANSLATOR'S INTRODUCTION

Clement, Beaufort notes, defines prayer as. . . . Clement of Alexandria (Henny Fiskå Hägg), pp. 132–135.

The text also corrects Beaufort's. . . . Gregory of Nazianzus (Martha Pollard Vinson), pp. 185–186.

Publishing his work required. . . . De Meester (1994), appendices II and III.

For more on the Quietist religious controversy, see these appendices, with letters by Beaufort, Fénelon, and other contemporaries who discuss it.

LAST WORDS

TRANSLATOR'S INTRODUCTION

This "goodbye" seems to have moved. . . . Because De Meester (1994) also refers to Letter 16 as containing this "goodbye" (see page 27, footnote 46), I went back to the earliest French editions several times to see if I had overlooked it, but there is no "*adieu*" in Letter 16.

LAST WORDS

Patience holds, considers, keeps. . . . Budziszewski, p. 58.

For more on the problematic word *perfect* (*perfectum*) in a theological context, as in this Latin version of James 1.4: "*patientia opus perfectum habet*" ("patience has a perfect work"), see Thomas Aquinas in *Virtue Ethics* and Budziszewski's point that *perfect* does not mean "flawless" here but the ongoing process of something or someone becoming "complete or fully developed," in other words, maturing spiritually, and becoming more loving.

TIMELINE

1628: "Without a summer".... Parker, pp. 7, 502; 3.
1628–1631: First bubonic plague.... Parker, pp. 630–31 (figure 3).
1640–1690: Little Ice Age.... Parker, pp. xiii, xvii.
1672: Extreme spring season drought.... Parker, p. 190.
1675: "Without a summer".... Parker, pp. 3, 7, 247, 336, 502.
1693–4: Historic weather takes many lives.... Parker, p. 589.

ACKNOWLEDGMENTS

The Bears on campus teach me so much. So do the squirrels, but that's another story. I'm lucky to learn from amazing students. Thank you for who you are and who you are becoming. You inspire me. You work bravely to make the world a kinder place. Thank you for honoring your voice. Honor your voice always. *Go forth and conquer!*

I want to thank Kamilah Newton for entering my life one out-of-the-blue-phone-call day, for a ten-minute interview that turned into a two-hour conversation, with a new friend, and I want to recognize Erinn Wong, because your good heart, strong research, and diligent revision crafted the excellent research project that brought this lifestyle writer at Yahoo! and Women's Prison Association graduate into both our lives. Kamilah, for your superlative articles articulating what matters and what needs to change so the Black community can experience equity, rights, and peace, thank you.

Lil Copan at Broadleaf Press, thank you for being my friend, for sharing creativity and brilliance, for being a book maven, and kind, and for recommending books, to read and to write, that grow my empathy. You started this adventure. "What about translating *Presence*?" you said, one of many bright ideas. That word, *presence,* stayed lit in me through 2020 and beyond, familiar like a night-light keeping me company in the dark.

I especially want to thank my colleagues in the College Writing Programs at UC Berkeley, who took me in when I was without an academic home. Your friendship, conversations, community, and shared pedagogy, also homemade wine, delicious low-acid coffee, lunch samosas at Lower Sproul, warm homemade apple pie in Oakland, Thornebrook chocolates, and Mountain Fireweed honey, have saved my life.

I also want to express my gratitude to Philip Averay, host of *Wisdom's Table*, and Amy Frykholm, host of *In Search Of*, for good conversations about Brother Lawrence and *The Cloud of Unknowing*. Their podcasts are in Further Reading and Listening.

I appreciate that Kamilah Newton introduced me to Diana McHugh, who helped make my invitation a reality so that a donation from the proceeds of each *Presence* book goes directly to the important nonprofit, the Women's Prison Association in New York City. Rebecca Pak, thank you for continuing that good work.

I can't thank these next people enough. They waded through when the waters were deep. I owe Shima Bagheri Ahranjani, Phyllis Duhon, Mary Grover, Ben McFry, Kamilah Newton, Toby Lee See, and several anonymous readers. Your gifts of time and close attention made all the difference. Our dialogue and your feedback improved this book tremendously. Thank you for being as kind as you are incredibly smart and equally wise. You delivered. Any weaknesses in it remain mine.

I have deep gratitude for the Bibliothèque Nationale de France for publishing the digital versions of the original texts, and for granting generous, free access. Thank you. Also, when I needed help with page 429 of the 1699 edition of *Presence*, Cédric Hourçourigaray emailed me right back with a solution on a bright-blue day in May.

Sean has helped me write books for so long now, by being there, always, that there is no thank you wide and deep enough, just love, and Lucky, our nineteen-year-old cat, sage by his long silence, still teaches us wisdom.

Nicolas Herman, thank you for your invisible heavy lifting, and for your presence. It's been an honor and deep joy to live with, puzzle over, look up, re-see, and steep in all the wise clues you left, and in your kindness. *Merci, mon ami bien-aimé.*